Common Sense Real Estate

Common Sense Real Estate

NEAL OCHSNER

AN OWL BOOK
HENRY HOLT AND COMPANY □ □ NEW YORK

To Janine

Foreword © 1990 by Neal Ochsner
Copyright © 1987 by Neal Ochsner
All rights reserved, including the right to reproduce
this book or portions thereof in any form.
Published by Henry Holt and Company, Inc.,
115 West 18th Street, New York, New York 10011.
Published in Canada by Fitzhenry & Whiteside Limited,
195 Allstate Parkway, Markham, Ontario L3R 4T8.

Library of Congress Cataloging-in-Publication Data
Ochsner, Neal.
Common sense real estate.
1. Real estate investment. 2. Real estate business.
I. Title.
HD1382.5.036   1987   332.63′24   87–8420
ISBN 0-8050-0509-9
ISBN 0-8050-1155-2 (An Owl Book: pbk.)

Henry Holt books are available at special discounts
for bulk purchases for sales promotions, premiums,
fund-raising, or educational use. Special editions
or book excerpts can also be created to specification.

For details contact:
Special Sales Director
Henry Holt and Company, Inc.
115 West 18th Street
New York, New York 10011

First published in hardcover by Henry Holt and Company, Inc.,
in 1987.

First Owl Book Edition—1990

Designed by Victoria Hartman
Printed in the United States of America
3   5   7   9   10   8   6   4   2

Contents

Acknowledgments

All real estate professionals develop a great part of their philosophy and technique through their experience with various properties and with other professionals. Properties shall remain nameless, but I would like to mention a number of individuals with whom I have enjoyed especially warm associations: Jay Anderson, Trent Chambers, Leo Frantzman, Mitchell Hochberg, Rick Kaufman, George Markus, David Mesker, and my brother, Andy. These excellent professionals epitomize the "common sense real estate investor," and have enriched this book by comment and example.

Special gratitude is due my agent, Blanche Gregory, and my editor, Jack Macrae of Henry Holt, who honed my themes and made this a better book than it would otherwise have been.

Finally, a loving thank you to the person closest and dearest to me, Janine, without whose help, comments, and ideas there would be no book at all.

Foreword

The first edition of this book appeared just a few weeks before the stock market plunged on October 19, 1987. In addition to signaling the end of a long, dramatic bull market, that drop marked the beginning of a new experience for Wall Street. At first, the markets were characterized by unprecedented stock price volatility coupled with record trading volume. Once so-called "program" or computer-driven trading was curbed, the exchanges settled down to an almost dismal level of business, punctuated by occasional flashes of the violent seesaw that had driven small investors from the market and confounded the experts. Despite the excitement that comes with periodic upticks in the Dow (nobody wants to take a chance on missing the next bull market), it seems likely that it will be some time before the stock market enjoys a sustained bout of solid, renewed investor confidence.

What Does This Mean for Real Estate?

One of the major themes of this book is that, properly selected, real estate can be a highly stable and predictable form of investment. In the 1987 crash, real estate stocks dropped far less than did the overall market. In uncertain times, people have traditionally sought property, finding comfort in its tangible nature. The drawback to real estate has not been less profit than the stock market, but less liquidity. You simply cannot sell real estate by calling your broker for the latest bid.

One reason to buy General Motors, Merck, or any other blue chip stock is because they offer liquidity, together with a history of stable, consistent growth. In a newly volatile stock market, the likelihood of that safety is severely diminished. How attractive is liquidity if a tenth to a third of your market value can erode in a few hours of frenzied trading? I am not saying that a person shouldn't have money in the stock market; I am just pointing out that one's stock portfolio used to be considered "safe," and that assumption may not be as true as it once was.

The Result is a Wonderful Opportunity

Since the October 19th crash, the new element in people's decision making is *uncertainty*. Uncertainty is keeping people on the sidelines of the stock market as it has dampened the market for almost all financial products and led to substantial layoffs on Wall Street. This same uncertainty has fed a soft real estate market. As a friend told me recently, "The only shortages out there are of tenants and buyers." The soft market may initially have been caused by tax reform and overbuilding, but heading into the 90s it is being prolonged by uncertainty on the part of businesses who may be reluctant to expand into new space, as well as individuals who are nervous about committing large sums of money to a first or larger home. If they lost money in the stock market, their nervousness is that much more acute.

Ironically, this may be precisely the time to buy. Properties are not selling quickly, and motivated sellers may discount heavily from their asking prices for a serious buyer. At the same time, there are signs that both interest and inflation rates may increase, which is bad for most of the world but is usually good for real estate values. Basically, real estate is a cyclical market and we may be at a low point in the current cycle. Investor uncertainty does not create distressed properties—just distressed sellers. That is the time to buy.

It doesn't matter that the recovery will probably be gradual. Real estate is a good place for your money to be while you wait. If you buy properly, the home or income-producing property you acquire will hold or appreciate in value. The potential exists to make a great deal of money. In the meantime, you will have a great deal more control over your assets and destiny than you would if your money was at the mercy of the stock market. Real estate is unique precisely because it affords a buyer the opportunity to *eliminate* many potential areas of uncertainty. This is not an easy thing to do, but you don't have to be an expert either. *Anybody* can do it, armed with common sense, patience, and a little basic knowledge about real estate. The purpose of this book is to help provide the tools you need to start you on a path towards high-profit, low-risk investment in real estate. I hope you enjoy the trip.

Common Sense Real Estate

"Common sense is not so common."
—Voltaire

INTRODUCTION

Why Real Estate?

America has always been fascinated by real estate.

Building is associated with the nation's earliest aspirations. Pioneers hewing a homestead from the wilderness, the hustle and bustle of far-flung outposts serving as the commercial center for entire territories, the erection of the first skyscrapers in the dawning of the industrial age, and, in the years following World War II, the dotting of the landscape with single-family homes—these are symbols of achievement and prosperity at the heart of our heritage. Real estate has epitomized the American Dream, that through hard work and virtue any man or woman can achieve success and property.

Many, many people successfully invest in real estate, and a significant number of them become very wealthy in the course of doing so. The fortunes of 101 of the individuals and families listed in the 1988 Forbes 400, Malcolm Forbes's annual list of the richest people in America, were ascribed to real estate; that's 26 more than were ascribed to all areas of manufacturing put together.

Thousands have enjoyed success on a lesser scale, ranging from those who barely miss inclusion in the Forbes list to common folk looking for a little extra cash.

The inspiration for many seekers—both successful and unsuccessful—has been the often-promoted gospel of "Get rich quick." It is the example of success in the real estate industry that has spawned the success of the real estate *book* industry.

Self-help books in real estate are not new. In 1959, William Nickerson wrote *How I Turned $1,000 into a Million in Real Estate—in My Spare Time.* The title of Nickerson's book makes it clear he is advising the common investor how he can become wealthy in real estate. With varying mixtures of confidence-building, legitimate basics, and oversimplification, this same message has been promoted time and time again over the years in books with titles such as *Nothing Down, How to Go from Rags to Riches in Real Estate,* and *The Courage to Be Rich.* As real estate has boomed, the books have boomed. A great many of the middle-class Americans who have made money in real estate succeeded because of wisdom gleaned from these books.

Unfortunately, "a book does not an investment make." High-leverage investing (the primary way one acquires real estate with no money down) is also high-risk investing. Many have lost money in real estate, confirming the bad impression many people have about the industry. The simple fact of the matter is that one *cannot* turn a dollar (or a *hundred* dollars) into a million without *risking* a great deal more. The cry of the real estate promoter is not unlike that of the used-car salesman, but with a bigger, more expensive product. *Would you trust this man?*

Buying properties is not an *easy* way to riches. Yet, if one were to believe real estate brokers and syndicators, they might well conclude that there is no such thing as a bad or overpriced property in *any* market at *any* time. *All* real estate is *always* a bargain. As Will Rogers pointed out, "They ain't making any more of it." Get it while it lasts.

For a long time this seemed like sound advice. The explosion of activity in American cities and suburban areas in this century has been something to behold—over sixty million housing starts from 1950 through the present, a figure accounting for most of the residential space in this country.

Cities spread like puddles, until metropolitan areas on the East Coast and elsewhere melded into one large urban lake.

While America has enjoyed what is clearly—on an overall basis—a tremendous real estate boom, it has been periodically marred by significant busts. In the mid-1970s, downtown city shopping districts were decimated as strong local merchants and shoppers deserted their streets to be in regional and super-regional shopping centers, placed at the intersections of major highways with a choice of department stores and literally hundreds of chain-store specialty shops; new tax incentives for historic rehabilitation have helped in major metropolitan areas, but midsized cities continue to struggle. The press of a decade later is filled with stories of cities such as Houston and Denver, where overbuilding has exacerbated the woes of economic downturns in the oil industry that sustains them. The syndication of high-priced, limited-partnership interests in these same buildings to thousands of investors across the country raised serious questions about the propriety of such investment offerings.

Such events lead to disenchantment.

Few of the "real estate rich" are recognizable as the traditional names of American wealth. Once this may have been accepted as proof of the American Dream. Instead, more obvious was the long-standing populist distrust of the very wealthy. It was as if they were robber barons, a suspicion confirmed by the perception—not entirely untrue—that those with the highest incomes, and particularly those in real estate, paid no taxes at all. It was the Corrupt American Dream, the achievement of success through shortcuts, without the requisite hard work and fair play.

This sentiment was clearly perceived by Congress as the Tax Reform Act of 1986 was debated. Eliminating the favored tax status accorded to real estate was first and foremost a simple matter of mathematics. To achieve meaningful tax simplification, which was broadly defined as fewer tax brackets at significantly lower rates, it was necessary to find *$100 billion* in deductions which could be eliminated. Historically, real estate was the single largest source of deductions, and it

was easy to conclude that the most visible representatives of
the industry looked a little *too* healthy.

In the final bill, 60 percent of the shifted tax burden fell
on real estate ownership. The most important means by which
this was accomplished was the elimination of interest deductibility and prohibitions on recognizing losses in the year they
occur. Previously, these provisions formed the foundation for
the financial structure of virtually all real estate investment
by individuals (as opposed to investment by corporations and
pension funds).

So-called "tax shelters," with write-offs nearing or exceeding one's investment in a property, are but fond memories
now, out-of-production relics soon forgotten in a few short
years of transition rules. Truthfully, this was not a great loss,
as the industry was already moving away from such transactions and would have soon abandoned them altogether even
without the shotgun encouragement of tax reform.

Still, there is no denying that certain benefits of real estate
investment, which were in effect subsidized by the old tax
system, are now reduced or gone. Inevitably, this eliminates
a component of value that was once part of a property's purchase price or appraised value. Such developments have
served to take some of the glitter out of property investment.

Despite setbacks suffered by the industry (and by some investors), real estate remains a powerful aphrodisiac for an
inordinately large portion of the population. Justifiably so.
Here are nine of the most compelling reasons why real estate
is regarded as the fast road to the top:

1. *Real estate and everyman.* Nothing beats success and
your own experience when it comes to picking an investment.
The experience of the American people with their own homes
has been the single biggest factor in popularizing real estate.
From 1965 to 1985, the price of the average home rose four-
fold, a compounded increase of 7.4 percent annually. That is
30 percent greater than the rate of inflation in the same period. In urban areas the increase was even more pronounced.
More recently, tens of thousands have reaped unexpected

profits from the conversion of their rental apartments to condominiums and cooperatives, often earning more than
$50,000 with the stroke of a pen. With an estimated profit of
$30 billion annually on an investment where appreciation po-
tential was not even the primary factor in the original decision to purchase, is it any wonder that everyone and their
neighbor feel they can make money in real estate?

2. *Good enough for the wealthy.* Think about the symbols
of wealth in profiles of the rich as they are chronicled in various magazines: a millionaire posed in front of his huge
Southampton mansion, a second with a regional mall sprawling behind him, a third wearing a hard hat on a catwalk
suspended high above the city. The rich and their real estate:
a common image. And not totally untrue. It was already
pointed out that over 25 percent of the families listed in the
Forbes 400 attribute their wealth at least partially to real
estate. It is a safe bet that not one of the four hundred—and
the next four thousand families—does not have real estate as
part of their investment portfolio. If *they* do it, *I* should do
it. Follow-the-leader is a game learned early in childhood.
Nothing about tax reform or periodic market weakness
changes the fact that real estate throws off money. Big money.
And appreciation. The tax benefits of real estate may not be
what they once were, but its raw earning power is un-
touched.

3. *The hedge that pays.* Real estate is a potent inflation
hedge. When times are bad, gold and real estate increase in
value. Of the two, only real estate generates income on the
way up. The main reason real estate functions as an inflation
hedge is that leases are either short-term (and are therefore
increased to reflect inflation as they turn over) or contain provisions that pass increases in expenses through to the tenants
while increases in rent accrue to the owner. During the extended bout of high inflation which we have only recently
left behind, many a poor investment decision was saved by
the beneficial effect of inflation on property performance and

values. With recurrent inflation an often-expressed possibility, real estate is at worst a sound diversification move and at best promises dynamic performance when you need it most.

4. *Outperforming the alternatives.* The plain fact is that real estate has significantly outperformed most investment alternatives. Table 1 compares the yields from 1970 to 1985 for real estate (performance of PRISA, Equitable's huge real estate fund) with those for common stocks, long-term bonds, Treasury bills, the average hourly wage index, and the consumer price index. Look at that real estate line break away as it heads up and off the chart. It is an eloquent argument for real estate investment. One picture says a thousand words.

5. *The inflation hedge in a period of disinflation.* Real estate is sometimes derided as an investment of the past. It was an outstanding performer during the high-inflation economy of years past, but what sizzle did it have left in a period of disinflation? This is not a fair or accurate criticism. First, it is necessary to understand that disinflation is *not* a reduction in prices; it is a reduction *in the rate of increase* of prices. Consider the following table showing the rate of inflation in an eight-year period from 1978 to 1985, and the "real" (inflation-adjusted) return from real estate investments in those years:

	Inflation Rate (%)	Real Return From Real Estate (%)
1978	9.0	4.5
1979	13.3	2.5
1980	12.4	3.5
1981	8.9	7.2
1982	3.9	7.9
1983	3.8	8.7
1984	4.0	8.3
1985	3.8	6.4

Source: Pension Real Estate Services, Inc.

TABLE 1

Real Estate: Outperforming the Alternatives

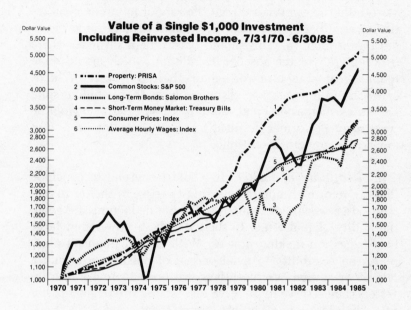

Value of a Single $1,000 Investment Including Reinvested Income, 7/31/70 - 6/30/85

1 ▪▬▪▬ Property: PRISA
2 ━━━ Common Stocks: S&P 500
3 ▪▪▪▪▪▪▪▪ Long-Term Bonds: Salomon Brothers
4 ─ ─ ─ Short-Term Money Market: Treasury Bills
5 ───── Consumer Prices: Index
6 ········· Average Hourly Wages: Index

The summary of investment performance shown above only compares the average annual return of stocks, bonds, Treasury bills, and real estate for a specified time period. There are other factors which must be considered when comparing different investment mediums, such as the relative degree of risk, liquidity, marketability, whether the investment is protected by insurance, and quality of management. None of these factors are taken into consideration in the graph above.

Source: Goldman Sachs Research

The second four-year period marks the beginning of a period of disinflation. Notice that in these years, the real return from real estate was *greater* than during the high inflation years (an average return of 7.8 percent in 1982–1985 compared to 4.4 percent in 1978–1981) and that *only* during the second period did these returns *exceed* the rate of inflation. Real estate as an inflation-adjusted investment actually fared better during disinflation. This should hardly be a surprise—there is nothing about the absence of inflation which should serve to make real estate fare worse than other investments. Whether we are in for inflation, disinflation, or that nebulous state known as stagflation, real estate is a consistent, nonvolatile investment performer destined to occupy a major portion of any serious investor's portfolio.

6. *A little bit of shelter.* It would be wrong to conclude that tax reform eliminated every last vestige of shelter in real estate. In a world where almost all other deductions are gone, the ability of real estate to shelter its cash flow looms large in the decision-making process. With careful financial planning, the possibility to avail oneself of passive losses and a few other special tax incentives still open to real estate investors should serve to preserve real estate's privileged tax status, albeit in a lower tax-rate environment.

7. *A hell of a lot of real estate.* In the Beginning There Was Real Estate. That's right. God had to create the earth before he could populate it with mankind, so the only thing Adam and Eve had to contemplate—other than the heavens and each other—was the site of all those future planned communities, suburban shopping malls, and gas stations. With sufficient cash or the right banking connections, they would have made a killing. As it was, a bad apple disrupted any development plans they may have had and there was plenty of land available for future generations. And all of it is different. Down every highway, street, and alley there is a building. Or several. In between there is vacant land calling

out to the developer hiding inside so many of us. The fact that real estate surrounds us—that we can never escape it—helps to keep it on our minds. Most of us do not know a transistor from a chip and will therefore not consider careers in electronics, but we all know the difference between an office building and a strip center. That awareness and accessibility insures that most of us at least consider real estate investment at one time or another. Lack of product and lack of comprehension are probably the greatest barriers to entry in any industry, and both are missing from real estate. That alone would make real estate a popular area for investment.

8. *Control in a world out of control.* Finally, real estate provides a little recognized, but powerful, appeal in its *tangibility* and human scale. We watch helplessly as stock investments jerk up and down on invisible puppet strings, as the value of the dollar mysteriously drifts against other currencies, or as interest rates respond to "macro" conditions readable only by economists and bankers. Ours is a world where the individual is increasingly out of control, at the mercy of forces beyond our knowledge and influence. It is difficult to commit our precious, hard-earned assets to such an unpredictable black hole. Real estate is different. You can *see* it, *touch* it. The forces affecting a property can, to a large extent, be fathomed. *Real estate offers an opportunity to regain control of one's assets.*

9. *Real estate runs itself.* Not exactly, but it certainly doesn't require constant care. It is tenants and customers, not owners, who constitute the day-to-day activity of a property. The first "business" of real estate is the provision of shelter, a basically passive activity. Even large real estate concerns can operate with just a few people. I once worked at a twelve-person firm with real estate assets exceeding *a billion dollars.* Success in real estate does not require that it be one's primary occupation (at least in terms of *time*). Thousands have earned

fortunes in real estate using it only as a part-time, after-hours avocation.

These factors combine to make a persuasive case for real estate.

The reality is that considerable wealth can be accumulated in real estate, but that get-rich-quick books, with their blithe, formulaic approach to property investment, do not offer adequate answers to investors. Today's real estate market is characterized by its diverse, constantly changing nature. No mere formula can hope to meet the demands of this environment. Success in an ever-changing financial landscape requires a solid foundation of investment skills and practices, used as the springboard to develop strategies responsive to the needs and opportunities of the moment.

Properly done, real estate investment is capable of providing returns far superior to those available in alternative investments, at a fraction of the risk. I am not referring to one narrow strategy for real estate investment, such as buying at foreclosure auctions or renovating old homes. Regardless of the real estate in which you are interested—whether it is an income-producing property such as an apartment building or shopping center, your own home, or even the publicly traded stock of a real estate development company—the same principles of real estate investment can be applied to earn consistent profit. This book will explain those principles, show how to recognize the existence of the real estate investment opportunities present in any market, and provide you with the techniques needed to realize the profit to be made in those opportunities.

This is organized in five parts.

Part I, "Understanding Real Estate," is just that: a common sense approach to demystifying and understanding the fundamentals of real estate investment. Investment strategies used by the top professionals in the business are described, together with a blueprint for finding accessible profit opportunities in *any* real estate market.

The purpose of Part II, "Investing in Real Estate Yourself," is to build on the concepts and strategies outlined in Part I by providing practical advice in the day-to-day nuts and bolts of real estate investment. If you want to purchase real estate directly, it is explained how to buy, manage, and mortgage a property or portfolio.

If you lack the time or inclination for direct investment, Part III, "Investing in Real Estate Through Others," lays out the investment alternatives for indirect participation through the syndication and stock markets, together with the means to find the sponsors, properties, and investment vehicles most likely to appreciate in value.

Part IV, "The Investment You Live In," deals with the biggest investment most people ever make—their home. How to find and buy a home which will hold and increase its value is discussed, together with the tax rules affecting home ownership, advice for second-home buyers, and the special considerations for condominium or cooperative apartment living.

Part V, "Building Wealth in Real Estate," shows how real estate investment should fit in with your overall financial planning. If you already own real estate, adjustments may be necessary to maximize its value. In some cases, real estate investment can enable you to shelter a substantial portion of a large income even though "shelter" supposedly no longer exists. Others will want more from real estate. Excellent investment opportunities may appear readily, but, if necessary, you will want to create your *own* real estate boom. In any event, it is important to find the right investment or investments for you, whether real estate is intended to be a small part of a diversified portfolio or a major means to real wealth.

Common Sense Real Estate is intended to act as a guide through the wilderness. Those who tame that wilderness will discover a golden city filled with treasure, theirs for the taking. Still, fortunes are made more often than found. It is not enough to simply know that profitable, attractive investments surround us. It is my goal to supply the tools needed to harvest the profit present in this or *any* market. The time has come for investors to reclaim control over their fortunes, and real estate is the way to do it. The opportunities are there, waiting for whoever is brave enough and quick enough to reach out and grab them.

Part I

Understanding Real Estate

CHAPTER 1

Basics

What is Real Estate?

Having answered the question "Why real estate?" it is useful to ask the question, *"What* is real estate?" The full answer is not as obvious as it seems.

Most of us can easily differentiate between what is generally deemed real estate and what is not. Houses, buildings of all kinds, parking lots, and building lots are all real estate. Boats, airplanes, and anything that might be sold off the shelf of a department store are among the items which are certainly *not* real estate. There are borderline items which are difficult to classify, such as agricultural land, air rights, and even billboards—all of which have certain characteristics of real estate and which we shall discuss later—but most of the time it is not important for us to decide whether or not these things are technically real estate.

We can all identify real estate, but what is trickier—and more immediately important if one is going to invest in real estate—is how real estate *functions*. What is the engine that drives real estate?

This answers the question "What is real estate?" in the same way that describing the mechanism inside a clock explains what a timepiece is. If one is to be a watchmaker, such knowledge is far more important than being able to identify a clock.

From a functional standpoint, real estate is either land or a structure, generally immovable, built on land. Either can also be described as *property*.

The purpose of property is some sort of *use*. There are obviously an infinite number of uses for real estate, limited only by the number of activities in which mankind engages.

It is the *use* of a property which allows us to make the first crucial differentiation between various kinds of real estate: *Owner-use* real estate is used by its owner or intended for owner-use; *other-use* real estate is used by others or intended for use by others.

It is easy to understand the purpose of and motivation for owner-use. Some activity—personal or business—must be conducted, and a place is required to do it. The commonest example of owner-use is the single-family detached house. The use is to live one's life in privacy and beneath secure shelter. The next-most-common category is businesses which own their own manufacturing warehouse or office facilities.

The second category—other-use—is no more difficult to explain. Properties in this category are typically known as income-producing properties. The motivation for other-use is generally profit. This profit is accomplished when the owner acts as intermediary between a property and its ultimate user. The link for this bridge is the *lease*.

The simplest and most basic real estate transaction is therefore the leasing or renting of a property from owner (lessor) to user (lessee). Starting with the lease as the basic unit of real estate operation, it is possible to construct a complete picture of how real estate functions.

The medium we will use to draw this picture is a *property income statement*. Other ways of describing property activity are available, but none which are so well suited to conveying the profit motivation underlying operations.

Before we begin on the property income statement, we must collect the leases we have signed and prepare a *rent roll*. This is a summary of the most important information on the leases and will, at a minimum, contain the following: the lessee's (tenant's) name; the space being leased (measured in square footage or designated by apartment/space number); and the rent (expressed in the manner in which it is paid—e.g., monthly, semiannually—and generally summarized for convenience as an annual number). Other information is often included for use in making decisions and planning, such as length of the lease, renewal periods, and other terms we shall discuss, but these are not the most important. The finished rent roll is organized in columns and looks like this:

HAPPYSHOP CENTER
Rent Roll at December 31, 1987

Tenant	Sq. Ft.	Monthly Rent	Annual Rent
Pa's Paws Pet Store	450	$150	$1,800
Sudsy Laundromat	450	150	1,800
Nickel 'n Dime Variety Store	1,000	300	3,600
Triple-X Market	2,000	500	6,000

So that the rent roll will provide a more complete look at what is happening at the property, we add three more lines:

Total Occupied	3,900	1,100	13,200
Vacant	450		
Total Center	4,350	$1,100	$13,200

The addition of occupancy and vacancy information puts property performance in perspective relative to property *potential*.

We are now ready to begin a property income statement for the year 1987.

The first line of the income statement is the total rental revenue paid by lessees to the lessor for their use of the property:

HAPPYSHOP CENTER
1987 Income Statement

Revenue
Rent $13,200

Note that: (1) Regardless of the number of tenants, rent is consolidated on a single line; (2) unless otherwise noted, income statements are almost always *annual*; and (3) unless specifically noted, an income statement should report only what has actually been paid or incurred, ignoring the potential income to be generated in vacant space.

It is rare for the income statement to end after the line for rent, as most property owners incur expenses. There are many levels of detail which could be shown when reporting expenses, but so long as a detailed record is maintained somewhere, major categories will suffice for the statement:

Maintenance and Repairs
Utilities
Real Estate Taxes
Insurance
Management Fee
General and Administrative

Of these, maintenance and utility categories in particular will be comprised of many smaller items—e.g., snow removal, salaries, etc.—some of which may be worth listing separately for some properties.

Adding expenses and calculating the difference creates an income statement that looks like this:

HAPPYSHOP CENTER
1987 Income Statement

Revenue		
Rent		$13,200
Expenses		
Maintenance and Repairs	$3,300	
Utilities	1,800	
Real Estate Taxes	2,110	
Insurance	870	
Management Fee	660	
General and Administrative	500	
Total Expenses		9,240
Net Operating Income		$3,960

This is not a complete income statement. A complete statement would include the effects of items such as depreciation, which are of critical importance to owners and investors alike. Our partial income statement takes us only through property operations, and is therefore more appropriately called an *operating statement.*

Used in conjunction with the rent roll, our operating statement gives us a good understanding of how real estate functions. To get a better understanding, we shall review the differences in use and leasing structures between the major categories of properties. We will then be able to return to the income statement and complete it.

The Major Types of Properties

It has always been a mystery to me why so few books on real estate investment take the time to explain the difference between the major categories of properties. This is a simple thing to do, and it is essential, since each property type has a unique set of financial return and risk characteristics. If one hopes to make choices between diverse investment opportunities and to then assume ownership of a particular property, he or she must understand the differences between property types, which are as much a part of a property as the frame of the building.

Single-Family Home

The single-family home—or simply, house—is the most basic and enduring element of the real estate scene, so much so that it needs no description.

The house is set apart from other forms of real estate by its simplicity in most matters. In contrast to most property types, it is generally owner-occupied and therefore usually involves no lease and no month-to-month profit motivation. The owner generally looks for three things from a house: (1) day-to-day use, (2) preservation of value, and (3) appreciation in value. These goals are so universally accepted that the single-family home is the only form of non-income-producing property for which nonrecourse mortgages (secured only by the property) are readily available.

Part IV, "The Investment You Live In," is dedicated to detailed discussion of various aspects of home purchase and ownership.

On those occasions when a house is rented, however, we have an easier time seeing how it fits into the larger context of property ownership. A house can be rented for many reasons, ranging from a temporary transfer out of town to the owner's desire to run it as a vehicle for profit. The typical house lease will be for either a fixed period of time or on a month-to-month basis, depending on the owner's goals in renting and whether he or she anticipates reclaiming the house for his or her own use at some point in the future. Rent will be a fixed amount, payable "monthly in advance" (payable at the beginning of the month), as opposed to "monthly in arrears" (payable at the end of the month).

The lease will most often be "net," meaning that the tenant bears almost all costs of upkeep. This usually includes electricity and other utilities (real estate taxes and insurance may or may not be paid by the tenant; if *all* expenses are borne by the tenant, the lease is "triple net") and *all ordinary maintenance expenses*. Such expenses would include snow removal, minor plumbing repairs, and—if the lease is for a significant period of time—painting. It would *not* include roof replacement, electrical rewiring, major plumbing overhauls, and other major capital expenses which are not due to tenant negligence or the ordinary wear and tear of time.

Leases usually provide for a house to be returned in the same condition in which it is initially leased. Disagreements over what constitutes "same condition" and "ordinary maintenance" are the basis for most home rental disputes. In deteriorating circumstances, the landlord may hold onto tenant deposits or the tenant may attempt to withhold rent, possibly bringing the entire matter to lawsuits and prolonged litigation.

In contrast to the example we have built up of a typical

operating statement, the single-family house is just a one-line statement—rent—with a one-line rent roll defining its entire structure. Herein lies a clue to the major peril in renting a single-family house—it is a one-lease, nondiversified asset. If your tenant withholds rent, sues, or skips town, you are without income until you can reclaim possession and get a new paying tenant. If damage has been done, you may have to bear the cost of repair yourself. After all, if the tenant was highly solvent and stable, he or she might very well be owning instead of renting.

The only ways to mitigate this risk are to carefully screen your tenants, to have a lease which clearly and unambiguously lays out the obligations of each party, to document the condition of the house in advance of the lease, and to pray.

Apartments

If you have ever lived in an apartment building, you probably understand how it works. From the owner's standpoint, it is not much more complicated than renting a house, but it is done on a larger scale. Sometimes it is a little larger; often it is much larger.

Tenants sign leases, usually six to twelve months in length. Utility costs, such as gas or electric, may be included in the rent or may be billed separately to tenants. Other operating expenses, such as grounds maintenance and real estate taxes, are invariably borne by the landlord.

Since there are many leases, the loss of one tenant—or a few—is not so devastating to cash flow as in the rental of a single-family home. By the same token, the more apartments you own, the more certain it becomes that you will have vacancies at any given point in time. You have mitigated the risk of zero occupancy, but you have also effectively given up *full* occupancy. This is a small sacrifice to make, all things considered.

Tenant turnover tends to be higher in apartment buildings than in other types of real estate. This again has both favorable and negative aspects.

In markets with high apartment demand, low vacancy levels, and increasing rents, this structure is very advantageous and profitable. It enables the owner to maintain a high average rent level with minimal risk of losing tenants. Also, expenses in such markets rarely keep pace or move with increasing income, meaning that the additional rent revenue is almost pure profit.

In weak markets, high tenant turnover means high vacancies. Here, rent levels are static or declining, giveaways—such as free washers and dryers or several months of free rent—erode profitability, and shorter leases further undermine the dependability of income. Under such circumstances, apartments, particularly complexes, have high expenses relative to income, creating the possibility for extended operating deficits in weak apartment markets.

The operating statement and rent roll for an apartment building are very similar to the models we constructed at the beginning of the chapter.

Office Buildings

In terms of physical plant, an office building tends to be far simpler than residential properties. While an office may be a converted house or apartment, architectural detail, kitchens, extra bathrooms, and even closets are generally superfluous. For that reason, most of the money in modern office construction goes into a sleek modern look, a fancy wrapper for the space to be leased. Office buildings are generally less expensive to build than residential properties.

Office leases tend to be longer than those for residential properties, averaging three to five years in length and often granting renewal options to tenants. This is so a tenant will have an incentive to improve and decorate his or her space without fear of eviction or massive rent increases.

Most office leases have a very important additional feature: *expense stops*. An expense stop basically provides that a tenant will pay his or her share of the increases in certain expenses (real estate taxes, utilities, insurance, and sometimes even maintenance costs) above the cost in the year in which the tenant moves in, called the *base* year. The share paid by the tenant is the percentage of square feet he or she leases relative to the total square footage of the property. Expense stops imply a very significant change in property operating statements. *There is an additional line of revenue.*

Changes to the rent roll are also necessary for this document to continue to be of assistance. It must now include the stop and base year for each tenant and expense category. In addition, we must have a record of property expenses in each base year.

Suppose 135 Rexall Lane is a medical office building with three tenants. This is the rent roll:

135 Rexall Lane
Rent Roll at December 31, 1987

Tenant	Sq. Ft.	Expense Stops (R. E. Tax)	(Maint.)	Rent (Mo.)	(Ann.)
N. Caine, DDS	500	1985	1985	400	4,800
A. Pill, MD	500	1986	1986	450	5,400
The Orthopedic Group	1,000	1985	——	700	8,400
Total Occupied	2,000			1,550	18,600
Vacant	500				
Total Building	2,500			1,550	18,600

We need to calculate expense stops for 1987. The expense history is as follows:

	1985	1986	1987
Real Estate Taxes	2,000	2,200	2,700
Maintenance	1,500	2,000	2,300

Each tenant pays his or her share of the increase in expenses above the cost in their base year:

135 Rexall Lane
1987 Expense Stop Worksheet

Tenant/Expenses		Increase Over Base	Expense Share (%)	Reimbursement
Caine	R. E. Taxes	$700	20	$140
	Maint.	800	20	160
Pill	R. E. Taxes	500	20	100
	Maint.	300	20	60
Or. Group	R. E. Taxes	700	40	280
	TOTAL			$740

Note that expense reimbursements, also called expense recoveries, are calculated on a tenant's share of *total* property area, not just the occupied area.

Our modified operating statement looks like this:

135 Rexall Lane
1987 Operating Statement

Revenue		
Rent	$18,600	
Reimbursements	740	
Total Revenue		$19,340
Expenses		
Maintenance and Repairs	2,300	
Utilities	1,200	
Real Estate Taxes	2,700	
Insurance	1,000	
Management Fee	930	
General and Administrative	250	
Total Expenses		8,380
Net Operating Income		$10,960

The expense stop is more than just an additional source of revenue. By buffering an owner from expense increases which would cut into profits (since revenues may largely be fixed by extended leases), expense stops provide an important hedge against inflation.

The combination of longer leases with controls on expenses serves to make office buildings a more stable form of real estate than apartment buildings.

Shopping Centers

Shopping centers are the most sophisticated of the "pure" real estate forms, both physically and in terms of their lease structure.

Shopping center technology has developed optimal store depths, layouts which maximize street exposure, parking ratios (the number of parking spaces per thousand square feet of store area) and ideal parking angles, lighting systems, and even theories about which types of stores generate the most shopper traffic at given locations.

This is not surprising since even the simplest shopping center is part theater. We have evolved beyond the bland definition of a shopping center as a shelter for retail shopping to a value system in which the best shopping center is one which *enhances* retail shopping. By becoming an active ingredient in attracting customers, the shopping center improves the profitability of its tenants and increases its own value as a property.

This role as a partner in the retail business raises the status of the shopping center and makes it less of a commodity than other forms of real estate. The center is not "just another shelter." A successful individual or company will move his or her or its residence or office to a better neighborhood; a successful store will more often just open an additional *outlet*.

This gives the shopping center—particularly the *good* shopping center—increased leverage in negotiating lease terms. Out of this situation developed two refinements to shopping center leases: expense *passthrough* and *percentage rent*.

Passthroughs are more complete versions of expense stops; instead of collecting a reimbursement for the increase in expenses over a base year, a tenant pays his or her share of *all* costs in major expense categories.

Passthroughs can be interpreted as a result of shopping centers being more important to the tenant than an office building, but the concept of percentage rent is a significant departure from all we have discussed thus far, reflecting the manner in which the shopping center *intrudes* and becomes a part of a merchant's business.

Percentage rent lease clauses obligate a merchant to pay a percentage of his or her store's gross sales. The shopping center owner avoids becoming a participant in a bad business by combining the percentage rent with a *minimum rent,* also called *base rent.* Therefore, a tenant pays the minimum rent only until sales reach *breakpoint,* typically the level where the percentage rent rate applied to gross sales equals the minimum rent. Therefore, a store with $15,000 annual minimum rent and a 5-percent percentage rent reaches its breakpoint at gross sales of $300,000. Percentage rent payments on sales over this level are known as *overage.*

Passthroughs and percentage rents have profound impacts on the property operating statement. Four columns need to be added to our original rent roll for Happyshop Center:

HAPPYSHOP CENTER
Rent Roll at December 31, 1987

Tenant	Sq. Ft.	Minimum Monthly	Rent Annual	Percentage Rent		
				Rate(%)	'87 Sales	Brkpt.	Overage
Pa's Paws	450	$150	$1,800	5	$65,000	$36,000	$1,450
Sudsy	450	150	1,800	5	30,000	36,000	0
Nickel 'n Dime	1,000	300	3,600	4	125,000	90,000	1,400
Triple-X	2,000	500	6,000	2	350,000	300,000	1,000
Total Occupancy	3,900	1,100	13,200				3,850
Vacant	450						
Total Center	4,350	$1,100	$13,200				$3,850

Percentage rents add $3,850 to revenues. Notice that even
though Triple-X Market is the largest tenant with the greatest
sales above its breakpoint ($50,000), it pays the lowest per-
centage rent rate and, with the exception of Sudsy Laundromat (which should probably be replaced when its lease
expires) has the lowest overage rent payment. This is because
larger tenants usually command more favorable lease terms
due to their ability to attract customers (and therefore, tenants) to the overall center. Triple-X Market is not large as
tenants and supermarkets go, but is large for Happyshop Center and acts as its "anchor" tenant.

The expense reimbursement calculation is simpler than that
for expense stops. Assume all tenants except Triple-X pay full
reimbursement on real estate taxes, utilities, maintenance,
and insurance. Those expenses add up to $8,080.

HAPPYSHOP CENTER
1987 Expense Reimbursement Worksheet

Tenant	Expense Share (%)	Reimbursement
Pa's Paws	10.34	$836
Sudsy	10.34	836
Nickel 'n Dime	23.00	1,857
Total	43.68	$3,529

Arithmetic in charts may not be exact because figures are rounded off. General
industry practice is to use exact math but also to show dollars and percentages
in either whole figures or rounded off to not more than two decimal places.

Over 40 percent of expenses in reimbursable categories are
recovered and *over a third* of all expenses.

Consider the final operating statement for Happyshop:

Calculating the impact of percentage rents and expense reimbursements (on page 28) increases Happyshop's net operating
income from $3,960 to $11,339, *a 186-percent increase*.

Because of these features, shopping centers are powerful
inflation hedges. Not only do rising expenses get passed
through to the tenant, but the effect of inflation on sales vol-

HAPPYSHOP CENTER
1987 Income Statement

Revenue		
Minimum Rent	$13,200	
Percentage Rent	3,850	
Reimbursements	3,529	
Total Revenue		$20,579
Expenses		
Maintenance and Repairs	3,300	
Utilities	1,800	
Real Estate Taxes	2,110	
Insurance	870	
Management Fee	660	
General and Administrative	500	
Total Expenses		9,240
Net Operating Income		$11,339

umes serves to increase rents. Even in deflationary periods, percentage rents offer a means to participate in any successful business which is a part of the center. Since rents are tied to sales rather than to profit, the center owner is unconcerned about a merchant's profit margins. With minimum rents protecting the downside, the shopping center becomes a partner with all of the benefits and few of the risks of retail sales.

This does not mean that shopping centers are without risks. High competition can make it hard to negotiate favorable leases and—worse—result in high vacancy. Still, in most situations, shopping centers—which often require little day-to-day management—have a lower break-even level than either apartments or office buildings. The opportunities for increasing shopping center profits are in raising rents and fine-tuning a center's tenant mix, lease structure, and appeal.

Hybrids, Pseudo–Real Estate, and Other Property Types
There are other types of property.

Multitenant industrial properties operate in much the same manner as office buildings, albeit with different physical considerations, expense ratios, and rent levels.

Single-tenant buildings of any type are often net or triple-net leases, commercial versions of the single-line operating statement we used for the single-family home, but with very extended lease terms.

Then there are a variety of property types which are hybrids, combining different types of property, or pseudo–real estate, combining attributes of real estate with other businesses.

Mini-warehouses are one example of a hybrid. They are a cross between industrial properties and apartments, renting small storage spaces to individuals on a month-to-month basis. Physically, mini-warehouses resemble industrial properties, but the on-site management, security, and leasing facilities required resemble those of apartments. Mini-warehouses are basically apartment buildings which rent only closets. Ironically, a primary motivation for many mini-warehouse investors is that inexpensive building costs make these properties an excellent means of speculating in land while still earning a current investment return, further proof of mini-warehouses' hybrid nature.

Hotels are the ideal example of pseudo–real estate, mixing real estate with other types of business. Hotels occupy a fixed building and offer what are in effect nightly leases, but are so management-intensive and encompass so many services (e.g., restaurants, bars, shops, and the special business of furnished-room rental and maintenance itself) that they are really a specialized business form in themselves. Oddly, hotel operators rarely consider themselves to be in real estate, but many real estate people aspire to the hotel business (often failing miserably when they fail to appreciate the special business needs). Also, hotel financing is virtually identical to and is considered but a single part of real estate financing.

Retirement congregate housing is in many ways a blend between hotels and apartment complexes. Such facilities are basically conventional apartment complexes with the provision of extra services, such as a meal plan, maid service, and social activities.

Even billboard rental has been considered a form of real estate, even though it is not a "property" in the traditional sense. Still, it does involve the rental of land or of the billboard itself, and the transaction employs a lease with specific terms. This may be more akin to real estate than other pseudo–real estate forms.

There seem to be fewer and fewer "pure" property types in real estate. Multi-use properties combining office, commercial, and hotel facilities, specialty shopping centers, and a host of other innovations, all serve to blur the lines between categories of real estate, and between real estate and other types of enterprise.

It is the success of real estate investment which has driven this trend. As real estate has thrived, investors have looked outward, justifying their expansion into other categories of real estate and into other businesses by attempting to claim that these new ventures are merely logical extensions of their own brier patch. This is fine, so long as one recognizes what one is doing.

What Is Real Estate Investment?

Now that we know how real estate functions and can recognize it in its many forms, we can reconcile the profit motivation in real estate operations with the business of real estate investment.

Operating a property to produce a profit is but one aspect of real estate investment. There are two basic ways to make money in real estate: *cash flow* and *appreciation* (an increase in value over time). Each of these corresponds to an investment activity: cash flow to operation, and appreciation to sale. For example, profiting from land investment is focused on appreciation realized at sale, as land does not require operation and does not throw off cash flow.

The value and increasing value of land is for the most part a function of a parcel's potential for development activity. Development, the building of a property, is another form of appreciation. The difference between the actual construction cost and the value of the finished property is profit from appreciation. If the property—whatever type it may be—is sold upon completion, then the appreciation has been realized and cashed in.

However, if the property is held or if an individual buys a property which is already completed, then the pursuit of profit becomes twofold, as the property begins to operate and the owner seeks both cash flow *and* appreciation. These goals are not in conflict, since increasing the cash flow of a property is the best means to increase its value, creating further appreciation over one's original investment.

There are other means to invest in real estate, but all are related in some way to either cash flow or appreciation. For example, the income a lender realizes on a mortgage comes from property cash flow. The purchase or sale of air rights is an attempt to realize appreciation in a specialized component of a property's value. Therefore, it should be clear that all real estate investment transactions come back in some way or another to the operation of a property or to the potential appreciation of an operating property, built or unbuilt.

This compels us to pick up where we left off on the property income statement. An investor is concerned with more than revenues, expenses, and net operating income.

It was at net operating income that we ended our operating statement. This described the functioning and activity of real estate, with all of its variations by property type. What lies beyond?

There are two elements of real estate which serve to further isolate properties from other types of investment: *debt service* and *depreciation*. Both of these are present in all businesses, but they are of particular importance for real estate. To see how they work, we need to link the day-to-day operating activity described in the operating statement to an owner's *investment* in a property. This link is accomplished by adding a new financial statement: the *balance sheet*.

A simplified balance sheet for Happyshop Center, if acquired at the start of 1987, might look something like this:

HAPPYSHOP CENTER
Balance Sheet at January 1, 1987

Assets		
Building	$120,000	
Land	20,000	
Total Assets		$140,000
Liabilities		
Mortgage	$112,000	
Equity	28,000	
Total Liabilities		$140,000

This balance sheet would mean that the property was bought for $140,000. $120,000 was allocated to the building and $20,000 to the land for depreciation purposes. Also, the purchase was 80 percent financed through a $112,000 mortgage with $28,000 balance paid in cash.

The information on both depreciation and debt service must now be incorporated into the property income statement. First, we will look at debt service.

Assume the $112,000 loan on Happyshop requires interest only and is not currently amortizing (repaying principal). If the interest rate is 9 percent, annual debt service is $10,080.

The simplified income statement for the first year of ownership is therefore:

HAPPYSHOP CENTER
1987 Income Statement

Revenue	$20,579
Less: Expenses	(9,240)
Net Operating Income	11,339
Less: Debt Service	(10,080)
Net Cash Flow	$1,259

Annual cash flow of $1,259 is hardly sufficient reason to invest $28,000 in a property. Clearly, we are looking for something more. That something more is increasing the cash flow through raising rents and realizing property appreciation when we finally go to sell the property.

There is also something else.

Buildings depreciate. This means that a property supposedly wears out over time, giving rise to an accounting convention—depreciation—allowing the investor to deduct the amount of his loss over time. If the value of a property was $100,000 and the depreciable life (a period set by law which has varied greatly and should continue to do so) was twenty-five years at the time it was acquired, then it would be possible to deduct $4,000 in depreciation expense per year. This is a *non-cash expense* and may have little basis in reality. In practice, real estate has tended to increase in value over time. *Real estate is the only investment in which you can depreciate an appreciating asset.*

We have said that Happyshop was acquired on or around January 1, 1987. At that time, the depreciable life for commercial properties was 31.5 years. With a depreciable base in the building of $120,000, annual depreciation is $3,810. Add this to the income statement:

HAPPYSHOP CENTER
1987 Income Statement

Revenue	$20,579
Less: Expenses	(9,240)
Net Operating Income	11,339
Less: Debt Service	(10,080)
Net Cash Flow	1,259
Less: Depreciation	(3,810)
Net Taxable Income (Loss)	$(2,551)

The net taxable *loss* is $2,551. The Tax Code has restrictions on the use of this loss, but if we owned Happyshop (which is not a large property) directly, or if we had what is called passive income, most of us would be able to deduct this amount from other income. (More complete discussion of the tax laws affecting real estate is provided in chapter 13, "Planning and Profiting Post-Tax Reform.") In a 28-percent tax bracket, this loss would reduce taxes by $714. Also, the $1,259 net cash flow would be tax-free. Therefore, our total annual benefit would be $1,259 plus $714, or $1,973, a 7-percent tax-free return on investment.

This is still not a staggering yield.

To see the power of real estate investment at work, we need to stretch out the property income statement horizontally, *over time.*

Assume that tenant sales and expenses at Happyshop Center increase 5 percent annually, and that the 450-square-foot vacancy is filled at the beginning of 1988 with a tenant who pays $2,500 annual minimum rent and who never reaches overages. The resulting five-year projection is shown in table 2 (sufficient information is provided for those who are interested to reproduce these results).

Seeing the effects of inflation, leasing, and leverage on property performance, we see our after-tax return on a $28,000 investment zoom from 7 percent to over 21 percent during a five-year period. This is the cash flow benefit of real estate.

Table 3, showing the effects of sale of Happyshop Center at the end of five years, completes the picture. After paying off the mortgage and taxes due on sale, one walks away with $57,338. This is $29,339 more than the original $28,000 equity investment, slightly more than a doubling of one's money. This is the appreciation benefit of real estate in addition to the cash flow benefits already enjoyed.

The overall investment in Happyshop represents approximately a 27-percent compounded after-tax investment yield. Do you know anywhere else you can get a sustained 27-percent annual after-tax return on your money?

Happyshop Center is not a large or unattainable property. The description and financial assumptions were not particu-

larly outrageous or aggressive. This is certainly an investment
which can be matched.

Armed with these basics of how real estate investments
work, let us explore how you can find investments which will
match or better this performance.

TABLE 2

HAPPYSHOP CENTER
Projected 5-Year Income Statement

Revenues	1987	1988	1989	1990	1991
Minimum Rent	$13,200	$15,700	$15,700	$15,700	$15,700
Percentage Rent	3,850	4,613	5,414	6,253	7,160
Reimbursements	3,529	4,583	4,812	5,053	5,305
Total Revenues	20,579	24,896	25,926	27,006	28,165
Less: Expenses	(9,240)	(9,702)	(10,187)	(10,696)	(11,231)
Net Operating Income	11,339	15,194	15,739	16,310	16,934
Less: Debt Service	(10,080)	(10,080)	(10,080)	(10,080)	(10,080)
Net Cash Flow	1,259	5,114	5,659	6,230	6,854
Less: Depreciation	(3,810)	(3,810)	(3,810)	(3,810)	(3,810)
Net Income (Loss)	(2,551)	1,304	1,849	2,420	3,044
Net Cash Flow	1,259	5,114	5,659	6,230	6,854
Tax Benefit (Cost) at 28%	714	(365)	(518)	(678)	(852)
Total After-Tax Benefit	$1,973	$4,749	$5,141	$5,552	$6,002
Return on Equity (%)	7.0%	17.0%	18.4%	19.8%	21.4%

TABLE 3

HAPPYSHOP CENTER
Effects of Sale at December 31, 1991

A. *Sale Price*	
1991 Net Operating Income	$16,934
Sale at 9% Capitalization Rate (the price where NOI equals a 9% yield to the new buyer)	$188,156
B. *Tax Basis*	
Original Purchase Price	$140,000
Less: Accumulated Depreciation	(19,050)
Adjusted Tax Basis	$120,950
C. *Tax on Gain*	
Sale Price	$188,156
Less: Tax Basis	(120,950)
Taxable Gain	$67,206
D. *Proceeds from Sale*	
Sale Price	$188,156
Less: Mortgage Repayment	(112,000)
Tax at 28%	(18,818)
Net Proceeds from Sale	$ 57,338
E. *Appreciation*	
Net Proceeds from Sale	$ 57,338
Less: Original Equity Investment	(28,000)
Appreciation Benefit	$ 29,338

CHAPTER 2

Common Sense Real Estate

The Meaning of Common Sense

The world has become a very confusing place. Nowhere is this more evident than in financial matters. Take the example of the traditional checking account: Not too many years ago a checking account required only that the customer make a record of his or her checks on an endstub or log as each was written, carry the appropriate balance forward, and then confirm the transactions when the monthly statement arrived. Interest on checking was neither expected nor available. Simple.

No more.

Today we have "total asset management" accounts, integrating checking privileges with money-market interest on funds; debit credit cards; cash advances; electronic transfers; credit lines; and very often, stock accounts. On opening such an account when they first became available, I discovered to my dismay that the endstub checkbook to which I was so accustomed was not even available.

From this morass of opportunity slip monthly statements the size of small magazines, with pages of computer printouts detailing transactions by chronology, type (e.g., credit card, checking) and effect on credit standing. Very often the account is divided into sub-accounts, making it nearly impossible to ascertain your true balance. It is easy in such a financial jungle to lose track of where cash stops and credit begins. One of the marketing directives behind these electronic candy stores is surely to make it so hard to keep track of funds that borrowing—which is made easy and pays far more handsomely than mere services for the institution in question—becomes far more likely.

However, it is not right that greater financial freedom, with its increased options and flexibility, be the occasion for anxiety and losing control of your financial management. *It is necessary to simplify the process.*

In the case of asset management accounts, this is done by keeping the traditional checking account log, and spending within the previous month's ending balance, with adjustments for any deposits during the month. Interest earned on the account during the month can wait until it appears on the next statement—plenty of time to spend it then. Credit cards can either not be used (you may prefer the float available on conventional non-debit cards) or used only for specific expense categories, and should always be logged as if a check was written. The effect of these measures is to break down the various flows of money into distinct components and slow down the apparent pace of spending.

This simplification process is the essence of common sense!

Webster's Dictionary defines common sense as "good sound ordinary sense." This is an excellent definition, as simple and plain as common sense itself. To try for a more specific definition runs against the meaning of the term, which is a powerful concept precisely because the ambiguity of the phrase allows it to encompass an important, bigger-than-life phenomenon.

Still, *Webster's* offers another definition:

> "Good judgment or prudence in estimating or managing affairs especially as free from emotional bias or intellectual subtlety or as not dependent on special or technical knowledge."

This definition captures the simplification process inherent in common sense. Emotionalism, complex logic, and special technicalities are all chased from the decision-making process. That is not to say that these things do not have a role in common sense investing, but they are secondary to the central question of whether an investment is fundamentally and intrinsically sound.

This brings us to a definition for common sense investing itself. Common sense investing is the simplification of complex decision making by reducing consideration of an investment question to a series of smaller fundamental issues, each of which is resolvable through plain, good sense.

Real estate is ideally suited to the common sense approach. Unlike the stock market, where perceptions of the market may control prices for extended periods of time and where companies are vast empires with a myriad of activities not easily researched or comprehended, investment in real estate tends to involve a single property with an inherent purpose (for example, it is clear that a structure constructed as a shopping center could never become an apartment building) and a relatively contained market. It is comparatively easy to come in and assess the true merits of the investment. Participation in real estate therefore *begins* with an important simplification.

The physical aspect of real estate reinforces the application of common sense. The ability to see and touch a property, to "kick the bricks," can quickly sober a rampant or hopeful imagination. It may seem trite, but the *real* in real estate is a quality worthy of a great deal of time and attention.

Unfortunately—or perhaps fortunately for us—people have gotten away from common sense real estate investing. In its place have come complex formulas for calculating returns, convoluted investment structures, and ambitious attempts to be the biggest or highest or most expensive something-or-other in a given market. Most of all, real estate has suffered through an extended period where undue emphasis was placed on tax benefits. Is the good investment the one that makes money or loses it? With the absence of most deductions, the answer is suddenly clear again.

It was fine and appropriate to ply legitimate deductions for all they were worth in the days of tax-incentivized investment, but those days are gone. With their demise, the advantages that once accrued to high-priced tax attorneys and accountants, or to those who would hire them, are also at an end. The Tax Specialist Is Dead—Long Live the Common Man. The playing field is level. Real estate is intelligible again. It is approachable and, with the diligent application of common sense investing, it will pay handsomely.

Bricks and Mortar

Armed with the fact (and it *is* fact) that real estate can be a good and understandable investment offering high-profit potential, it is not time to run to the nearest real estate broker with pen poised above open checkbook, ready to take the first apartment walk-up or office building you are offered. The opportunities in real estate investment exist only if you are prepared to make careful, informed property decisions (this is nothing more or less than common sense, a standard which will appear often in these pages). Unfortunately, available properties and information about them cannot be found as simply as stock market quotations in a newspaper's financial section. Such easy accessibility would preclude the possibility of the very situations being sought.

What is required is the careful application of basic real estate knowledge, skills, and strategies over time to yield attractive, profitable investment properties. This does not conflict with the exhortation to common sense investing. Far from it.

There can be no more appropriate analogy for real estate investment than the construction of a structure. Think of the components for successful real estate investing as a pyramid (not a modern shape, but a venerable one) with five levels. The first four levels are:

Level One: ⟶ Knowledge
Level Two: ⟶ Skills

Level Three: ⟶ A Strategic Plan
Level Four: ⟶ Execution

Level Five, the peak of the pyramid, is Profit, but the top cannot be set directly. Let it suffice for now that profit will come easily if you lay the first four levels properly.

All structures require building materials. Our pyramid is fashioned of two precious commodities—common sense and experience.

Common sense is the substance from which all the bricks are forged. It must permeate every step of the investment process. If something goes wrong with a project, it generally goes awry either where common sense was not used or where a brick was forgotten altogether.

Sometimes a risk you did anticipate will go against you. All investments involve some level of risk, and how much money you stand to gain is directly related to the level of loss you are willing to accept. The purpose of the investment process is to minimize the chances that these so-called *business risks* will occur and to insure that, if they *do* occur, your losses will be manageable. If you suffer losses due to something out of your control and could not afford that outcome, then you probably made a bad decision at some point along the way. One of the first rules of investment is always to insure the ability to fight again another day.

"Experience" is very simply the mortar that holds the bricks together. The more you use, the stronger your structure. Without mortar, it all depends on how carefully you lay the bricks. You must be that much more careful if what you build is going to hold. *Warning:* Don't build too high a structure without mortar. It will topple, in all likelihood after too much money has been irretrievably spent. If you have never bought real estate before, don't start with a development project or a strip center unless you have experts right at your side for every decision and step of the way. Start at the appropriate level for your experience and financial capacity and you will be fine. One good test is whether you feel comfortable with

every check you have to write. If you don't, question whether
you should make that investment.

Common sense *is* the investment pyramid. The next step is
to look in more detail at each level of the Common Sense
Pyramid, and in so doing provide a framework for top-notch
investment decisions.

A Foundation of Knowledge

You could spend every day of your life in real estate and
still not know everything about how a property functions.
The fact of the matter is you *have* spent every day of your
life in real estate. When you go to the shopping center, stay
at a hotel, show up at work, or return to your house or apartment, you are using real estate. Somebody built, owns, and
operates each one of these "projects." In the case of your
home, *you* may be the owner and operator. In any event, the
experiences you have in all of these places are the stuff of
which real estate decisions are made.

Why do you return to a particular shopping center? "I like
the wide choice of stores." You have described a *balanced
tenant mix.* "It is right on the highway." *Easy accessibility.*
"It has my favorite department store." *Strong tenant.* "Interesting things always happen there, like concerts or art shows."
Effective center promotion. Each of these factors is a valid
consideration in deciding whether to buy or how to operate
a property. The analysis of a prospective buyer begins with
trying to figure out the analysis of a prospective *user.* If you
don't feel safe at a property, then the landlord needs to figure
out a way to fix the problem, or he will lose you and all his
other customers or tenants. The same rule applies if you feel
a place is dirty or poorly maintained. People stop using a
place that they find unpleasant.

If you are going to invest in real estate yourself, the first
lesson is therefore to realize that the broadest and most important base of real estate knowledge you have is your experience as a *potential user.*

An investment banker I know has an MBA from Stanford.

For all her specialized business knowledge, she feels much more comfortable when she is working on companies with which she can identify. "Give me fudge factories and people who make toys for my dog," she says. "Aircraft parts and resistors bore me." She likes real estate because she can identify with it.

This does not imply you are the prototypical customer for every sound property, or that you should limit your investment only to real estate you would use yourself. Just because a person prefers luxury hotels does not mean there is not a very substantial market for discount motels. However, it does imply the necessity of being able to sometimes step out of Guccis and into good solid working boots in order to make an informed decision.

This is not an easy thing to do. For years, many people shunned investments in mini-warehouses, the drive-up facilities where individuals rent storage lockers by the month. These properties were invented in the Sunbelt, where the construction of houses without full basements left people without adequate storage space. They spread to urban areas and gained acceptance in the rest of the country, and are now a familiar sight across America. Mini-warehouses aren't pretty and they aren't for everyone, but those who invested early have profited handsomely, both from substantial tax-sheltered cash flow and from appreciation in land values, as many of these secondary locations were upgraded to higher, more profitable uses. Now that mini-warehouses have proved their investment worthiness, returns in future years are likely to be lower. Congregate-care facilities and other housing projects for the elderly, avoided by investors who consider it morbid to profit on what demographers are calling "the graying of America," may now be at the passage reached by mini-warehouses a decade ago.

There is a great deal of knowledge required for real estate investment which cannot be intuitively reached through identification with users. After all, the goals of users and owners are not always the same. Several years ago, when the peso was being devalued in Mexico, a major international bank sent me as its consultant to a resort hotel south of the border. Only a short time before, the resort had been one of the hang-outs for the international jet set, built by one of its members as a playground for his wealthy friends. It was still a beautiful place, but investigation soon showed that it had a terrible layout for efficient operation as a hotel. The sprawling placement of rooms combined with the poor placement of kitchen and housekeeping facilities—a bad "back of the house"—made for inefficient, costly operation. It was virtually impossible to deliver the high level of services required to maintain the proper clientele and still turn a profit. An idyllic setting to visit, but a losing proposition as an investment. It makes sense to look at the customer's point of view, but he who pays the bills has a higher, broader vista to consider.

The millionaire who built the resort managed to discover this while he was still a millionaire and sold the property at a profit to a multinational corporation who knew nothing about how to run a hotel. The multinational waged a pitched battle against soaring deficits and sinking quality. They lost. The company made two mistakes: First, they bought the project without adequately understanding how a hotel functions; and, second, they compounded their woes by trying to manage the resort themselves. It may have still been the millionaire's problem today had the multinational corporation hired people with the proper knowledge, who would have told them not to buy.

"I know nothing but the fact of my ignorance," said Socrates, whose great teaching was that the essence of wisdom is an awareness of what one does *not* know. Heed him well.

But just as awareness of how a property is used does not preclude consideration of how it is run, neither does a willingness to hire others where your knowledge is weak mean that you should know nothing.

Understanding the interaction among all the various players that together constitute an *industry* is essential if you want to become a part of that industry. Developers, syndicators, foreign buyers, institutional buyers, property managers, brokers, lenders, leasing agents, lawyers, accountants, consultants, appraisers, and others are all working—sometimes in unison, often in competition—to create real estate activity. This is the market. The market for Boise, Idaho, rarely touches the market for San Francisco, California, but discreet and sometimes surprising links can exist, whether it is the attractiveness of life in San Francisco that causes an executive to move his company from Idaho or the high prices in California that lead a syndicator to look for buildings in Boise.

Ignoring the more subtle flows of market forces can be every bit as dangerous as not understanding the market at all. If you lose your wallet, it really doesn't matter if you left it in a taxi or if it fell over the side of an ocean liner. In either case, it is most likely gone forever.

There are a lot of technical definitions and phenomena particular to real estate which a person must include in his base of knowledge in order to function as a real estate investor, but these can be readily learned. Many things—such as the meaning of percentage rent and the parts of a mortgage—are discussed in this book. These will all come in good time, as you read about real estate and get experience in the industry.

Market knowledge—an amalgam of rent levels, leasing practice, prevailing prices, and demographics—is much more important than what Huck Finn would call "book larnin' " in developing the foundation of knowledge, which is the first level of the Common Sense Pyramid.

This is information in flux, changing constantly as buildings in construction are opened, old leases expire, and new zoning ordinances are passed. If you are on vacation (or investment prospecting) in a city you have never visited, you may be struck by the evidence surrounding you of a tremendous building boom and a local economy bursting at the seams. Your rented car passes through a busy intersection where a new apartment complex is under construction. In your peripheral vision you see a vacant lot with a For Sale sign plunged into the ground. Mindless of the traffic, you slam on your brakes, thinking only of constructing a crisp one-story building with a stucco finish which you will populate with a convenience store, laundromat, pizza parlor, and shoe repair shop. What you may not be aware of is that the local builder of the apartment complex has a larger site nearby on which he will construct a larger shopping center, tenanted by a full-line supermarket and a discount department store. Furthermore, he has convinced the head of the town council—his brother-in-law—that the corner you wish to buy should be purchased by the city through eminent domain for use as a small park, which is the reason the current owner is attempting to sell the lot at what sounds to you like a reasonable price. Put that checkbook away.

It can be hard to get the information required for an informed investment decision, but it is worth the effort. When you identify an area in which you are interested, or even a particular building, start by suppressing all the reasons you should proceed and concentrate on developing an objective, comprehensive understanding of the market.

The first level of the Common Sense Pyramid—a foundation of knowledge about a property and its market—can never be too broad or too strong.

Every Number Tells a Story

The second level of the pyramid involves the application of investment skills to your real estate decision-making process.

There are a number of such skills required to make informed investment decisions, but the most important of these are the *financial* skills.

You may recall earlier references to hiring specialists such as engineers and lawyers to assist where your own knowledge is weak. The temptation is to rely on an appraiser to determine the purchase price for a property and an accountant to ascertain its profitability.

Never!

The heart of the investment decision is to choose whether

or not to spend your money, and to determine what return you can earn. These are the twin, but intertwined, questions of *value* and *yield*. Appraisers and accountants can provide information supportive of your decision-making process, but it is not possible to relegate resolution on these questions to others. *To do so is to lose control of your own money.* This would obviously be disastrous.

It is the job of an *appraiser* to determine the fair market value of a property as of a certain date. That is useful information, but it falls short of an investment decision in three ways:

1. *Value is not to be confused with purchase price.* The buyer is not interested in a *fair* price. He or she is after the *lowest* price.
2. *Market values change.* As a buyer, you are less interested in where the market *is* than where it *will go*.
3. *Appraisers determine a range of likely values.* Who hires an appraiser and for what purpose can influence final appraised value. The designation MAI (which really means "Member of Appraisal Institute") is often jokingly said to stand for "Made As Instructed."

Similarly, *accountants* record the historical and current financial condition of a property. Again, this is three conditions short of an investment decision:

1. *Accounting deals with transactions rather than judgments.* Nothing about the capital spent on a property suggests that it was worth it. Putting a new roof on a building neither makes that roof good nor says it added its cost to the value of a property.
2. *Financial statements look backward instead of forward.* It makes sense to know what a property *has done*, but it is the buyer who must determine what it *can* and *will do*.
3. *Accounting measures cost, not value.* This is not the sin-

gle biggest shortcoming of accounting for real estate investing. Through the mechanism of depreciation, accounting *reduces the cost of transactions in an attempt to simulate the effect of time on property*. In the real world, good investment decisions both add value above their cost and appreciate in value due to market and economic forces completely separate from transactions.

I do not point out these shortcomings of both appraisal and accounting for decision-making as condemnations of either discipline, as neither sets itself up to be a substitute for the investor. The error is made by the investor himself or herself in the way he or she delegates away that which is the final responsibility of the investor alone.

If the true standard for appraisal is fair market value and that for accounting is cost, then the guideline for an investor is *return*. All of the skills residing on the second level of the Common Sense Pyramid are attempts to determine the return a particular real estate opportunity offers.

There are two reasons that questions regarding return are so difficult to delegate to others. First, the measure of what constitutes an acceptable return varies with the needs of each individual. Second, the return available from an investment is a potential which varies not only with each property, but with the resources which one puts into it. Therefore, *return is characterized by its uniqueness*. Uniqueness of *need*, of *property*, and of *resources*. A decision embracing this triangle can be made only by the individual who will control all three of its points.

Determining the first corner of the triangle—the return *required* of an investment—will change with each investment. A property may provide a high return—say, the opportunity for doubling its value within a short time period—at an unacceptable risk. Assessing this risk/return relationship is what this entire book is about, and cannot be conveyed quickly.

The minimum return acceptable on an investment will depend on the return available from other investment and the type of investment dollar slated for real estate investment. If a tax-exempt municipal bond offers a 9-percent annual tax-free investment at moderate safety, it is clear you would require something more than a 9-percent after-tax yield to invest in real estate with its additional risk factors. If the money you intend to spend on real estate is your only source of income, you will require real estate with a dependable current cash flow and you will be limited in your choice of appropriate investment. In particular, you would be denied the most exciting aspect of real estate yields: *the potential for appreciation.*

The reason investors acquire a property and mortgage it to the point where debt service effectively saps all of its current cash flow, leaving them with a reduced equity investment paying no current dividend, is that the mortgage leverage can reduce the cash outlay required while amplifying the effect of appreciation. The goal is "more bang for the buck," as explained more fully in chapter 7, "A Borrower and a Lender Be." You do not need to understand how this is accomplished to see that the buyer who should acquire a property producing a current cash flow with modest appreciation potential is not the same person who should seek out opportunities with no current cash flow, but the potential for a big increase in value down the line.

The minimum yield you can accept is a function of (1) the overall yield you can make elsewhere, and (2) the flexibility you have in how that yield is realized, whether it be current cash flow or future potential for appreciation. Knowing what you *don't* want is the first step to knowing what you are seeking.

All of this should be accomplished before you ever set foot outside your home or office in search of a property. Once you find an investment opportunity, the much more exciting prospect of determining what it can yield begins. This is the second corner of the triangle.

You have studied the market and the property. You understand both intimately. What comes next?

You apply the financial skills referred to at the beginning of this section; first as a detective and then as a seer.

Existing properties will generally have historical operating statements, hopefully prepared by an accountant, but certainly verified by you and your professionals. In any event, there will be a history reflected in the operating results of competitive projects observed and gathered in the course of your market research.

As a detective, you have to find the sometimes hidden meanings in those numbers. Electric costs are low compared to comparable properties: *Does this mean the energy system is efficient, or that the old owners did not light the property sufficiently at night?* Every year there are receipts for patching the roof: *This is possible evidence that a new roof is required.* In a shopping center, reported sales of all tenants but one have increased steadily: *Should the single exception be removed when his lease expires, or, in a situation where his rent is a percentage of his sales, is he underreporting his sales?*

There should always be a link between financial and physical reality. The trick is not to take numbers for granted, but to seek out what they imply. Numbers are harbingers both of future risks and opportunities. Many people freeze up and panic when confronted with pages of numbers. Looking at them one at a time and probing to the underlying *activity* behind each figure removes a great deal of the threat such numbers offer in groups.

The numbers are of importance because money is the manner in which we regulate and keep track of investments and their returns. It is not enough to see that one out of four apartments requires new kitchen appliances. It is imperative to know the cost of those appliances, and by how much rent can be raised in those units. *Every story tells a number.*

Having worked detective-style from the numbers into the innermost workings of a property, it is necessary to go back from the physical realities to the financial implications. This is the *financial projection.*

The numbers in a financial projection should accurately reflect the physical and strategic plans for a property. As investor, you have gone from detective to seer. Perhaps more than seer, because you are not dealing merely in flights of imagination. You are crafting an alliance between currently obvious needs, future possibilities and probabilities, and the *resources* at your disposal—the third corner of the triangle.

It is not uncommon to see financial projections where income and expenses are escalated at 5 percent (or some other number) annually, throughout an extended projection period. To some extent this reliance on broad trends is necessary for lack of a precise idea what will happen in the future. However, certain costs and opportunities can be projected more accurately. In a shopping center or office building where leases are far below current rent levels, it makes sense to project forward to the point where those leases can be brought up to market rates. Similarly, insurance rates as a national trend and real estate tax assessment practices in most communities tend to be increasing at rates faster and slower, respectively, than other expense categories. To the extent each item on the income statement can be fine-tuned, projections become of increasing value in the decision process.

The danger in the flat escalation feature of projections is that they tend to make every deal work. Even if a projection is sufficiently detailed to reflect the cost of a union contract expiring in two years, or to disregard the benefit of several mild winters on snow removal expenses in years past, it will be inadequate if it fails to account for future softness in rents caused by the completion and introduction of competitive properties into the market.

Don't lose the forest for the trees. Attention to details is useless if it fails to account for the vagaries of larger forces buffeting the property.

These macro-risk factors cannot always be predicted as easily as the completion of a competitive property for which construction was underway when you purchased your property. Surprises may come in the form of competition announced after you have committed your capital or it may be the unexpected loss through bankruptcy of your largest tenant. If your investment is in a community dominated by one company or industry, it may be loss of residential tenants or sales through weakness and layoffs in that industry. There is always a great deal which cannot be predicted.

When the unfathomable occurs, you have to be able to weather the storm. This is where those crucial resources come into play. It is not enough to have money coming in from other sources or to know you have a reserve of other money available for emergency, although these things are also necessary. *You must be certain the investment process does not undercut your future resource planning.*

Suppose your projections show a gradual but steady increase in operating profits. It is tempting to let these profits be rolled back into the real estate to pay for next year's new generator or parking-lot repaving the year after. *Don't do it.* When setting the budget for property improvements which *must* be done, do not rely on projected profits to pay for them. Look at a zero- or negative-growth scenario. Can you still afford the property? What can reasonably go wrong? What can *unreasonably* go wrong? The same rule applies when you are deciding how much to borrow on a property. Just because a lender will give it to you does not mean you can afford it. You may not find this approach to real estate in the get-rich-quick books of years past, but it is better to get somewhere slowly than not to get there at all.

Having good financial skills is not knowing how to work a calculator. You can and will learn that easily. It is far more important that you develop good financial and analytical habits and attitudes. These are the skills that will make or break you.

Let us get to the next step of the pyramid.

Custom Investment Strategy

The third level of the Common Sense Pyramid is developing an investment strategy. You have the knowledge and skills to invest, but you lack the plan of attack to find and breach your dream properly.

Finding an investment strategy is like buying a suit. There

are two basic ways to buy a suit: off-the-rack or custom. Off-the-rack strategy is reading a how-to book or article espousing some particular method and then trying it. Like the off-the-rack suit, it may fit you or it may not. Custom strategy is fitted to you. It takes a little more time and comes a little dearer, but it works and is a thing to treasure forever. The most famous custom suits in the world are available on London's Savile Row. The tailors there lavish attention on every handmade detail, from the way the suit hangs off your shoulder to the buttons that actually work on your coat sleeves. The shops on Savile Row are known as *bespoke* tailors, and their individualized creations are famous as *bespoke* suits. Not everyone in the world will have a bespoke suit, but *you* shall have a bespoke investment strategy.

Investment strategy is the path followed to find and acquire a property suited to one's particular needs and resources. It is the internal consistency between the path and its individual constraints which make it bespoke. A perfectly fitted strategy goes beyond merely serving its purpose; it maximizes one's natural competitive advantages.

This concept starts from the premise that a given strategy is not equally appropriate for each person. The most obvious demonstration of this—not drawn from the real estate world—is that the person who is politically well connected has an easier time securing government contracts than one who knows nobody in political power. It may be that such a person started without contacts and developed them only to facilitate the pursuit of Uncle Sam's dollar, but it is more likely the reverse was true. Therefore, *the first measurement in a custom investment strategy is an assessment of one's strengths.*

Here are a few examples of strengths or resources which are effectively converted to strategy:

Connections: Keep your ear to the keyholes and pursue deals arising from the information you have ahead of others or which require political connections. You will be the one to acquire the vacant lot across from the new transit stop, and guess whose project will skip to the front of the line when exceptions are considered for the sewer hookup moratorium? It is unfortunate in a democratic land such as ours, but few competitive edges can be parlayed into greater success than knowing the right people.

Architectural or engineering skills. The dilapidated building on an otherwise good street can be a fearful sight to those without the technical knowledge to recognize the true extent of its problems. Don't buy the structure in *truly* bad condition—you give away your advantage if you buy something with which anyone would do equally well—or poorly. Keep looking until you find the property whose problems are resolved more easily than initially apparent. There are more than a few architects and engineers who have gone from employee to employer.

The patience of Job. There aren't a lot of bargains buried in the real estate classifieds, but there are some. He who has the patience and determination to slog through the trials of answering-machine messages, busy signals, and missed connections in order to visit scores of misrepresented investment "opportunities" and to analyze a hundred more before ever finding one worth buying (and which may not be buyable for what he is willing to pay)—*he* shall succeed admirably.

These are all valid strategies, but the approach suitable for most people is rarely that clear-cut or dramatic. The best place for most people to begin is with an assessment of their financial resources and the time they can give to their real estate ventures. It is obvious that the man with a nest egg of $20,000 to invest, and a full-time job in Chicago, does not begin in search of large shopping centers in Cincinnati. However, he might purchase a four-unit walk-up apartment building in his own suburb. Such a property will be easy to rent and maintain.

If he has a little more money, a little more time, and knows how to repair things, he might buy a six-unit apartment building in need of some work. Still more money and time, and a father-in-law in the construction business, and he might buy a vacant lot for development of a *ten*-unit building.

And so on and so forth.

The particular direction you select will be a function of your investment goals. If you want safety, stick with constructed and leased apartment units. If you can afford more risk—with a higher return—then try the fix-up or development.

Even without special investment skills, familiarity should help dictate the choice of strategy. Doctors will have an easier time with medical office buildings than they will with industrial "spec" space (space constructed without a tenant in mind, on a *speculative* basis). The reverse applies to the businessman who owns a company which manufactures and distributes insecticides.

An additional series of strategies are suggested by one's real estate skills themselves. Through market research, it is possible to identify markets where you would like to be or particular products in short supply within a market. Such conclusions may be reached through the feeling that an area does not have enough readily available shopping or by analysis of demographic statistics that show a shift to larger-sized households (calling for development of two- and three-bedroom apartments where studios and one-bedroom apartments dominate).

Demographic statistics and sociological trends are definitely an underutilized strategic thrust for those who would use this information to determine product needs or improve amenity packages. One excellent and successful product improvement which recently developed out of sociological analysis is the "mingles" unit, an apartment or home with two master bedrooms to accommodate the growing number of singles who become roommates far past the age and affluence level where this formerly occurred.

The ability to see the real estate market that doesn't exist yet is a time-honored skill in an industry that has been characterized by its flair for innovation. It is also an effective competitive edge, albeit one which entails more risk than plumbing the known, established markets for various forms of property and amenities. Suppose you build a product for which there is no market or which is too far ahead of its time? You may be hailed as an innovator, but your laurels will be of no value in bankruptcy court.

The Rouse Company is an excellent example of innovation strategy. Combining superb quality with inventive product design and concepts, Rouse has prospered as one of the premier developers in the nation, first of suburban shopping malls and later of the urban speciality center with historic or other tourist appeal, such as Boston's Fanueil Hall or Baltimore's Harborplace. What is not generally known or remembered by the general public is that this same Rouse Company was once severely strained by the financial burden of developing Columbia, Maryland, an ambitious "new city" project. Columbia eventually succeeded, but not until after its exorbitant carrying costs combined with the severe real estate market downturn in the early seventies to force Rouse to sell off joint-venture interests in a number of its lucrative shopping center holdings. Even the best of innovators can have their plans fall out of step with their resources.

In all likelihood, the investment strategy and competitive edge which is best for you will entail some combination of talents, skills, and approaches. In Career, the popular Parker Brothers board game, players pick the formula combining wealth, power, and fame which they will pursue throughout the game. The first player to achieve the points required in all areas of his formula wins the game. Real estate investment strategy is comparable. Rouse—a very successful company despite its Columbia setback—combined high quality with its penchant for innovation. The investor who patiently seeks out properties which have been underutilized or allowed to run down will also require the skills to correct those deficiencies. He or she who identifies a market which promises good future growth will need some means of locating affordable opportunities in that market.

It is not enough that the end product of custom strategy merely fit you, it must also look presentable to and be consistent with the world you live in. It is of little use to emphasize skills in industrial warehouse development if that market is severely overbuilt in the area where you plan to operate.

Like custom suits, custom strategy requires dozens, perhaps hundreds, of measurements. Well and correctly put in harmony, the end product can be a formidable force for profit. Take your time and assemble your strategy carefully, using the knowledge and skills acquired from earlier levels of the pyramid. Then, if the strategy fits, wear it.

The View from the Top

Onward and upward we climb, scaling the final levels of the Common Sense Pyramid. The higher we go, the more careful we must be to set the bricks squarely and mortar them solidly in place. To fail to do so is to invite collapse and, as we go higher, so do we have further to fall.

Appropriately, the next level of the pyramid is *execution*. Good execution is certainly not particular to real estate or even to investment, but is absolutely essential if you value the time and money at stake.

Very simply, the fourth level of the pyramid is the determination to be complete and careful in every task and step of the investment process. This leads to fewer mistakes and better decisions.

If you have ever been at the top of your game in any sport—whether it be tennis or soccer or chess—you know there comes a point of increased awareness and control where the action seems to slow down and you are able to smoothly, masterfully plan and execute the appropriate response. In such a state, play is easy and pleasurable and—much more often than not—you emerge the winner.

This is the condition you should be seeking in your investment activity.

When you feel rushed or pressured or lost you are far more

likely to make a mistake. It is essential that you feel in control of events rather than feeling events are in control of you. Achieving this comes back to the premise stated at the beginning of this chapter: *Common sense investing is the simplification of complex decision making by reducing consideration of an investment question to a series of smaller fundamental issues, each of which is resolvable through plain good sense.*

This simplification process has the effect of slowing the action and facilitating a considered, unrushed decision.

A common negotiating strategy employed by many people (perhaps even by yourself) is to force a quick response. This takes the form of short deadlines, ultimatums, bullying, and even just talking fast. It is important not to succumb to these tactics unless you are truly ready to proceed. In general, if the other guy is serious about negotiating an agreement, he will wait for your answer. It may be that forcing him to wait will unnerve or frustrate him and provide you with the edge he hoped to achieve over you.

No amount of care is undue in making investment decisions. It pays to verify and continually retest market conditions, numbers, deal terms, and the like. A mistake can be too expensive.

When I began in real estate investment, powerful hand-held calculators were just beginning to replace computer time-sharing systems for certain types of investment and value analysis (with the invention of the personal computer and spreadsheet programs, computers are again on the ascendancy). Our company, a pension fund–backed real estate investment trust, was preparing to bid for a major portfolio of regional shopping centers. The final bid—which had been prepared on a new calculator model purchased only a week earlier—was several hours from final submission when the executive vice president asked that the numbers be verified on the computer. The check revealed a *$60 million overbid,* caused by a mistake in how the calculator was used.

A $60 million error is not easily recognized on a half-billion-dollar transaction, but it is more than any company wishes to waste, and thus proves the necessity of continually checking and rechecking, challenging and rechallenging every assumption on which your investment decision is made. This means using both checks of arithmetic and tests against common sense. If you find you are paying $110 per square foot for a building that would cost only $70 per square foot to build, ask yourself whether this is appropriate. If no vacant land exists in the vicinity of the subject property, this may indeed make sense; if the area looks like a pasture with your intended acquisition in the middle, think again.

The reward for careful execution is stepping up to the final level of the Common Sense Pyramid: *profit*.

If you have done your job well on the lower levels of the pyramid, you should have no trouble reaping the benefits at the peak. The view from the top can be very nice indeed. Cash flow from your investment, the opportunity for appreciation, and the development of a successful track record all enhance one's chances of scaling the pyramid again and again, working from a secure position of strength.

Setting down a solid foundation, then building each level solidly on top of it, improves your odds of being able to lay that last golden brick of profit. If you aren't careful early on, all you will lay is an egg.

CHAPTER 3

Every Building a Business

What Properties and Seasons Have in Common

America destroys more buildings in a year than most countries build in a decade. Think about that for a moment. Our refuse and obsolescence, transported abroad, would be another nation's real estate boom. Most of these properties are not decrepit or failing structures; they are simply victims of an ever-changing landscape which demands that land be applied to its highest and best use. They are buildings out of step with the times.

Obviously, buildings do not begin out of step with the times. Something must change. Perhaps it is the building. Perhaps it is the times. Most likely, it is both.

Properties, like seasons, are characterized by their tendency to change. The concept which describes this phenomenon is known in real estate as the *property life cycle*. Understanding the life cycle is essential to understanding real estate.

The typical property moves through six phases over its history:

Phase 1: Raw Land
Phase 2: Development
Phase 3: Start-up

Phase 4: Stabilization
Phase 5: Decline
Phase 6: Redevelopment

As obvious as it may seem that a property begins as raw land, gets developed, and eventually ages to the point where it is in need of help, each of the life-cycle phases carries with it a particular set of risks and rewards.

Raw Land. When a prospective building site is but a vacant dirt lot, it is by no means a foregone conclusion that a property will eventually be developed at that site. Many a person has kicked himself for missing the chance to build on some parcel out of which a magnificent edifice has risen, but this is the wisdom that comes only with hindsight and is worth nothing at the bank.

In a given market area, land values tend to follow a relatively constant and flat trend until such time that reduced supply and increased demand significantly increase value. The trick is to buy as close as possible to the point when prices begin to take off. As a general rule, land must appreciate at least 15 percent annually to justify carrying costs, real estate taxes, and the opportunity cost on the money invested. The purpose of land speculation is to capitalize on rapid appreciation in value. The keys to success are good timing, the right location, and a soothsayer's understanding of urban growth patterns.

Development. Real estate developers make money the old-fashioned way—they *build* it. Unlike the land speculator, who relies on the market to increase the value of his or her investment, the developer tries to create value in excess of his or her cost by purchasing land and then constructing a property on it. The amount of profit is a function of market prices relative to building costs, and the amount of work the developer does (i.e., whether the land had to be rezoned or was development-ready). Risk in a development project depends on the ambitiousness of the construction undertaking, the amount of capital involved and whether it is borrowed or out of the developer's pocket, and the strength of the market. The best development projects are obviously those where cost is well below market value. The riskiest are those where competitors can acquire existing properties for less than the cost of new construction.

Start-up. Start-up is really part and parcel of the development process, although certain of the skills required for success are quite different. The start-up of the building—which in most types of real estate focuses on the lease-up of apartments, commercial space, or other building areas—is where most value is created, or forfeited. The speed and rent rates at which a building is leased determines the amount of operating deficits incurred during start-up, and the amount of profit once the break-even threshold is crossed. A strong lease-up can save a botched construction job, just as a weak lease-up will ruin the smoothest of developments. Real estate values are largely a function of cash flow; cash flow is a function of lease revenue and costs. Hence, lease-up is mighty important.

Stabilization. After start-up, most properties enter a relatively prolonged period of stable operation and occupancy. During this period, value increases at a slower pace, moving up or down with cash flow and the level of buyers' interest in that particular market or property type. It may be necessary to fine-tune management strategies, tenant mix, and turnover rates. The challenge for ownership during this period is to attain the maximum revenue and minimal costs while maintaining the property in sound competitive and physical condition.

Decline. Failure to keep a property in sound condition—whether through neglect, deferred maintenance, or inevitable obsolescence—brings a project into the fifth phase of the property life cycle. Decline may be out of ownership's control; new competition may be developed, neighborhood demographics may change. More often, certain measures can be taken to delay or put off decline. Eventually, nothing more can be done. The value of the asset is at stake. Ownership is faced with a choice: ride the property down into oblivion, sell it, or redevelop.

Redevelopment. Redevelopment can mean various things. In the case of a property which is tired but well located, it may constitute rehabilitation or renovation. This can range from a cosmetic fix-up to a gut renovation, saving nothing but the building shell. Expansion may save the competitive position of other properties. Where demographics have changed, leveling the old building and starting over from scratch may be the best alternative. If the area has improved, this may constitute a tremendous opportunity as land is upgraded to its highest and best use. The risks and rewards of redevelopment can be every bit as dramatic as those of the original development process.

Real estate eventually comes to this demand for renewal. This call is a challenge to creativity and can be quite a profitable undertaking to those who would pick up the gauntlet.

The stage of its life cycle where an investor acquires a property has a tremendous impact on the risks and returns he or she can anticipate. Real estate is not static. It is imperative that you recognize this if you have any intention of succeeding as a property investor.

Supply and Demand

There is no more basic economic concept than the law of supply and demand. Very simply, it says that if supply of a product goes up, demand—per unit—goes down. This also means that prices go down, as price is a function of demand. Conversely, if supply goes down, demand and prices increase.

Most often we think of supply and demand as applying to macroeconomic concepts such as the forces moving the value of the dollar or the prices of agricultural economies. If we think about it further, we acknowledge that supply and demand can be used by companies in the pricing of their products. However, it is rare for most of us to employ supply-and-demand analysis for our own investment decisions.

In the case of real estate, failing to apply supply-and-demand considerations is to omit the most fundamental, powerful analytical concept available for predicting property performance.

Because real estate is characterized by its fixed location, supply-related factors (i.e., the location, number and relative merits of other properties) have major—and often predictable—effects on demand-sensitive variables such as occupancy levels (though occupancy technically measures the supply of available space, it is clear that low demand would directly result in low occupancy levels), lease terms, and rent levels.

It is with this in mind that a prudent buyer should not only undertake a comprehensive market study in order to assess current supply/demand/price conditions, but also plot demographic trends which might affect demand, such as population growth, and track the expected absorption of market area space, taking into account the introduction of space under construction or in various planning stages.

Assessing supply-and-demand factors can be far more subtle than counting occupied units at a given point in time. In the Phoenix market, where summers can be excruciatingly hot, it is not uncommon for an apartment complex to be near full occupancy during the winter, with droves of residents walking away from their leases (and rented furniture) in the hotter months. A different phenomenon appeared in the Houston apartment rental markets at the height of the city's trouble: apartment-complex owners gave new residents one to three months of free rent to induce them to sign leases, only to find that these tenants would often disappear into the night with their possessions at the end of the gratis period. Occupancy reports showed near-full occupancy, but rent collections were minimal. Obviously, rent collections count for far more than mere occupancy levels. A proper use of supply and demand therefore requires possession of statistics and information which *accurately* reflect the true activity of a property.

Another simple but very powerful way in which supply and demand affects real estate is in terms of geographical considerations. The tools required to perform such analysis are nothing more than state and local maps.

The state map provides clues to the importance and stability of the city in which a property is located. Is it near other major cities? Do major highway and transit routes pass through the area? Is the property located between two cities whose growth might be expected to converge, filling in vacant land between the centers of commerce? Phoenix and Scottsdale, Miami and Fort Lauderdale, Dallas and Fort Worth, and the entire mid-Atlantic seaboard are examples of this very logical growth pattern.

Further data can be drawn from a local map to predict property viability.

Compare the market for residential property in Houston to that in Chicago. A hot market for years, Houston became the victim of weak oil prices and severe overbuilding. New properties were purchased well below their original costs, but even at low prices some of these properties remain years away from successfully leasing up. One reason is that Houston continues to grow, expanding ever outward in concentric circles as new properties are developed. At some point, new development will cease, but the sector that leases up first may not be the area in which you choose to invest. This contrasts sharply with Chicago, where two factors influencing the attractiveness of residential real estate are proximity to the downtown area and to Lake Michigan. There is good reason to believe that market forces will place upward pressure on the value of the fixed amount of real estate which satisfies both of these criteria.

Peter Morris of VMS Realty, a large syndication firm which manages over $5 billion worth of property, calls this "strategic investment," where a property or location can't be duplicated or has a monopoly on some desirable amenity, such as an especially nice beach for a resort hotel or a location at a major highway intersection for a shopping center. It is basically an emphasis on the supply-and-demand factors for real estate. In the Houston market, supply and demand are both expandable; in the Chicago example, supply is fixed and the outlook for increased demand is strong. I'll put my money on the second scenario every time.

Investing in beachfront land, industrial parks next to airports, and apartment complexes near public transportation and urban centers may seem obvious, but it is these properties which are in short supply. It is these properties which will be affected least by poor market conditions.

Applying laws of supply and demand to your investment decisions in this manner is essential if you are to recognize which properties are resilient to trouble—and which are not.

The Importance of Gut Feel

The property life cycle and supply-and-demand factors are only the most graphic illustrations of change and volatility in real estate. Properties also move in much subtler patterns. Every single property is different. Every piece of real estate is like a business, each in continuous competition with its neighbors. As properties come and go, as tenant mixes change, as labor costs rise and building systems wear out, so must these businesses cope.

The collective effect of these pressures creates *property dynamics*. This is the interaction (1) of properties with each other (really, *market* dynamics) and (2) of forces within a property. Some of these forces may have little to do with the real estate itself, such as financing or deal structure, although they are likely to have an impact on the way in which a property is operated.

In a very real sense, property dynamics constitute the *personality* of a property.

Let me give you some examples:

- A small shopping center has poor visibility and access. The only tenants which thrive are a kosher butcher, a bike shop, and a shoe-repair store. All are *destination* stores which do not rely on traffic volume.
- A suburban office building is across the street from a park. A computer consulting firm and law office are very happy tenants, but a telephone sales firm leaves because employees spend too much time in the park.
- An apartment complex is having trouble leasing up. Competitors are giving away one month of free rent, but the project has high mortgage debt service and a low operating deficit reserve for lease-up, leaving no room for leasing incentives.
- A bar in a dilapidated wharf area is thriving. It is next to a popular restaurant which has been there for half a century and is owned by a former police chief.

All of these cases convey the personality of the properties. They show their dynamics with the peculiarities of their environment. Many of these things could have (and may have) been anticipated by developers or buyers. All offer risks and opportunities for each property owner. Properly analyzed, the property dynamics in each case suggests the proper strategy for future development.

Sure, investment bankers and MBAs think about buzzwords like *property dynamics*, but what about the people who really make money in real estate? Is this sociological stuff used by the Taubmans, Zeckendorfs, and Helmsleys of the world?

Absolutely. They call it *gut feel*.

Gut feel is an important traditional concept in real estate. It describes an ability to instinctively understand real estate dynamics. It is an innate comprehension of how a property functions that comes partially from experience, but more from an intimate understanding of all factors that go into and affect a property. This means construction costs, operating expenses, rent levels, market conditions, competitive properties, and everything else you can think of.

I had the privilege of knowing the legendary Sol Goldman who, when he passed away in 1987, was the largest single owner of real estate in New York City. He could tell you the value of any building from Battery Park to 125th Street. Off the top of his head. *Without leaving his office.*

How did he do it? He lived and breathed New York real estate for half a century. He looked at thousands of buildings, owned and operated a fair percentage of that number, and was constantly aware of who was buying what from whom and for how much.

He had gut feel. He also had a wealth of knowledge from which to draw.

I have seen people witness similar displays of real estate expertise, only to conclude that they could never hope to compete against such a talent or to reach such a command of property. They lose their confidence and it impairs their ability to make decisions.

This is the wrong reaction.

The proper response is to realize that what we witness as snap decision making can, in slow motion, be broken down into a careful examination of the numbers and property conditions. It is less important to make a quick decision than to make the right decision. This is the common sense simplification process at work.

Your ability to master the dynamics of real estate and to understand how those dynamics translate into financial performance is the key to developing what others will see in you as a gut feel for real estate investment.

Real Estate Awareness

The legendary Scottish city of Brigadoon, made famous by Alan Jay Lerner and Frederick Loewe in their Broadway musical and Hollywood extravaganza of the same name, appeared for one day every one hundred years. You had to act fast to catch it.

The same is true of real estate opportunities.

If properties are changing—whether through the natural

course of the property life cycle or the forces of marketplace supply and demand factors—then it is logical that various investment opportunities will open and close over time.

These are windows which must be entered quickly if one is to be successful. The brevity of the opportunity is not due to the possibility that that property will keep evolving—real estate does not change *that* quickly—so much as it is caused by the inevitability that *someone else will grab the opportunity first*. As a result, it is necessary to *anticipate* change in the marketplace.

If yuppies are moving into a once fine neighborhood which has fallen on bad times, it is not necessary for the process of gentrification to be complete before you decide to participate in the urban reclamation. If you wait, prices will already have risen dramatically.

This much is obvious, but was it possible to have *anticipated* the renovation of the neighborhood even before the first pioneers arrived?

Here are some signs that might make a neighborhood a likely renovation prospect:

- Existing stock of run-down but good-quality housing, preferably with some architectural character.
- History of having once been a good neighborhood.
- Neighborhood adjacent to or in the path of area growth.
- At least one natural aesthetically attractive boundary, such as a lake or a park.
- Commutable distance to a healthy urban business center.
- Rising prices and/or overcrowding in existing "good" neighborhoods.
- Increasing commutation time to "growth" areas.
- Existence of government-sponsored loan, auction, or tax-abatement programs to encourage renovation.

Being an urban pioneer, either as a resident or just as an investor, is not for everyone, but this list reflects a way of looking for opportunities on the eve of their arrival. Similar approaches can be applied to identifying cities which are likely to enjoy good growth or to finding downtown manufacturing buildings which could be successfully converted to office space.

In a broader sense, this anticipatory outlook is required for *any* investment foray, if only to appreciate what will happen to the competitive environment in which any property exists.

The best investment opportunities may not be advertised in the real estate classifieds or listed with brokers. To succeed in real estate investment requires *real estate awareness*. People with real estate awareness are easy to spot. They walk down the street with their faces turned upward, watching new buildings go up and speculating on the possibilities for old buildings. They cause auto accidents because they are writing down the numbers on For Sale signs instead of watching the road. They wander onto construction sites, ruining the shine on their shoes or breaking heels.

The real estate aware are open to the possibilities and opportunities for change. As they consider investment possibilities, they develop a sense of what a property is, where it is going, and what it is capable of doing.

Developing real estate awareness is part of realizing that investment is fun.

CHAPTER 4

Pockets of Opportunity

The Biggest Market

According to the Securities and Exchange Commission, the total market value of the securities traded on the New York Stock Exchange at the end of 1984 was $823 billion. Adding all other major exchanges brought market value to $959 billion, less than $1 trillion. At the same point in time, the U.S. Bureau of Economics reported a total value for residential real estate exceeding $3 trillion. Nonresidential real estate constituted almost another $2 trillion. The real estate "market" is clearly our biggest forum for equity investment in America.

There is a tendency to speak of the real estate market as a single national whole. This is no more true than that there is a single economy, inflation rate, or even national spirit. Nothing in these concepts precludes a particular area of the country from flourishing while another is depressed, just as a generally good stock market does not mean all stocks have increased in value.

For that reason it becomes very clear that talk of a depressed real estate market does not mean that all real estate is depressed. This has never been the case and never will be. But the case for real estate investment goes much deeper than mere contrarian reasoning. It focuses on three issues:

1. Real estate is an "inefficient" market, with exceptional yields always available to those who seek them out
2. The only market that counts is the one in which you are active.
3. Real estate is characterized by "pockets of opportunity," superior real estate investments which exist in *all* markets at *all* times.

Understanding the forces behind these phenomena is essential to profitable real estate investment at any time.

The Meaning of Market Inefficiency

The size of the real estate market was not compared to that of the various stock exchanges just to show the extent by which the former dwarfs the latter. In many ways these "markets" are very different and comparison is inappropriate. However, one of these differences is a beacon which can direct us to superior values in real estate.

One of the fundamental concepts in modern portfolio theory is known to business-school students everywhere as the *efficient market hypothesis.* The first statement of efficient markets, which paved the way for all of modern portfolio theory, was by Harry Markowitz in 1952. The hypothesis essentially says that in the stock market at any point in time, share prices reflect all available information, including future expectations by the market.

A simple example of the efficient market hypothesis is a stock where a dividend has been issued consistently for many quarters in a row. Between dividends the value of the stock will rise gradually in anticipation of the next dividend, dropping again by the amount of the distribution as its record date is passed. Any information which would suggest an increase or decrease in this dividend, or otherwise affect the prospects for the company, would immediately be incorporated into the trading price of the stock.

Consider the tremendous implications of this theory: Future prices cannot be predicted from past price data . . . Share

values have no memory . . . Only new or shock information
will cause prices (which incorporate all other available data)
to change, but new information cannot be predicted and immediately results in price adjustment. As a result, it is not
possible to use public information to make excess returns. In
the absence of insider or truly superior information, the best
one can do over time in the stock market is the overall performance of the market, less any selling commissions you have
paid.

Whether or not you like or accept this theory, you should
know that the efficient market hypothesis has been hotly—
and inconclusively—debated by academicians ever since it
was first stated over thirty years ago. If it is wrong, it is not
very wrong.

The tremendous implication of the efficient market hypothesis for real estate investment is that in contrast to the relatively efficient stock market, the real estate market is obviously
and unquestionably *inefficient.*

The sources of this inefficiency begin with the very vastness
of the real estate market and go on to make a long list. Some
of these inefficiencies include:

- Differences in the levels of return between various regions
  and property types
- Lack of information regarding prices and financial performance
- The existence of properties which are not being managed
  as well as they could be
- The lack of sophistication on the part of many sellers (and
  buyers)

Each of these factors constitutes an opportunity for the wary
and diligent investor.

Ironically, this situation prevails in an industry where
property performance is comparatively "efficient" and predictable. Without inordinate difficulty, the investor can accurately survey the supply of existing real estate, vacancy

levels, rental rates, and new construction, and assess the likely level of major expense categories, such as real estate taxes, insurance, utilities, labor, and even repair costs.

Predictable performance (to a point) and inefficient purchase and sale markets combine to make an attractive invitation to returns outpacing not only the stock market, but also that of the overall real estate market itself. It is by outperforming the market that the investor insulates himself or herself against unexpected downturns in performance and stays in position for exceptional profit when all goes as expected.

The Only Market That Counts

If you are in Cleveland, what do you care what happens to the real estate market in Denver, Dallas, San Francisco, or New York?

You don't.

Most investors never will—and never should—look beyond their own area for real estate investment opportunities. This is the market they know best and the one where they are likely to have the best access to information, sellers, and financing. Also, home is the market where it will be cheapest to mount both acquisition and management efforts. Very few investors have the time or money to go jetting off to distant cities in search of one or two extra percentage points in yield. The costs of doing so are certain to eat up these profits, and a great deal more.

In truth, you are no more likely to find those extra percentage points someplace else than in your own backyard. This is the case even if you reside in what is considered a weak or "soft" market.

In a weak market, the prices for real estate tend to drop. More specifically, *prices in a weak market drop enough so that the investor's initial yield is actually greater than in a strong market.* This supposedly compensates the investor for having the decreased upside potential associated with a weak market.

Weak market or strong, there will always be superior investment opportunities nearby. Consider the following combinations of national and local conditions:

Weak/strong. If the national market is perceived to be bad, it tars all markets. Even the strongest local market will be less robust in an environment where the *Wall Street Journal* has a steady flow of articles describing weakness in real estate. Investors tend to take any reason not to invest, even where it may not apply. This suggests that local properties may be underpriced.

Strong/weak. If real estate is considered strong nationally, almost all money tends to flow into a few markets. This is generally the building for the next big bust. If your area has a slow economy, it will barely benefit from booms in other cities. Prices are low, but justifiably so. Look for quality in your real estate. These properties will be the last to suffer and the first to prosper. In addition, they will be available at prices you may never see again.

The success of real estate ultimately depends on its use. So long as there are people in a market, some properties will enjoy strong unabated use. Those are the properties to own.

Weak/weak. The best of all market conditions for a buyer. Prices are depressed, so yields are up. With bad times factored into the price, you can afford to suffer. Markets such as these are far worse for those who bought property when prices were high than they are for those who buy at the bottom. Hopefully, there is only one way to go.

Strong/strong. The most dangerous time for a buyer of real estate. You don't want to miss the boom, but you don't want to buy at the top of the market. Consider sitting the market out, but if you must buy, look for the secondary benefits of a strong economy. This includes less-glamorous real estate such as industrial properties, or weaker market sectors where prices may not have taken off yet. Finding the right property in the market under a full head of steam requires hard work and high caution. Use your superior knowledge of the local market to find hidden values.

If this sounds like an overoptimistic or blithe approach to values, remember that *all* real estate investment should depend on exploitation of real estate's intrinsic tendency to inefficiency.

Pockets of Opportunity

Even in a slipping market, real estate opportunities abound. This is due to three factors, all already discussed. First, a downturn in the market—especially a market as large as real estate—does not mean the market is down in all places. Second, there are opportunities for taking advantage of market inefficiency. Third, there is a tendency for some buyers to stay out of what is perceived as a declining market. This is another form of market inefficiency, since these buyers are not present to compete for the bargains which remain.

The presence of market inefficiencies does not necessarily mean that bargains are readily available. Inefficiencies only reveal sources of opportunity which must then be capitalized upon. If the bargain was obvious or easy, it wouldn't exist.

As you might guess from the efficient market hypothesis, the first place to look for real estate bargains is where others fail to see them, *where you possess information not recognized by the person you are dealing with*. The best example of this is the classic "face-lift," where a property such as an apartment building has been allowed to run down and is attracting rents near the bottom of the market. The owner— either absentee, simply unaware of the potential, or unwilling to make the necessary upgrading investment—sells you the property on the basis of what it is rather than incorporating some of the upside potential into the purchase price. You then proceed to improve the maintenance, paint the halls, add some landscaping and perhaps building security, weed out unsavory tenants, and increase the rents accordingly. In

a few lucky circumstances, where the property is well maintained but the unsophisticated owner is not familiar with the
prevailing rent rates or property markets, you will be able to
go directly to raising the rents or collecting an above-market
return on your investment.

Other instances where your vision can be twenty-twenty
while those around you are shortsighted include *demographic
investing*, where you identify population growth or other demographic trends suggesting increasing demand for certain
markets or products; *Columbus investing*, where you go as
an explorer into neighborhoods which are still savage or don't
exist yet; and *sweat investing*, the creation of value through
hard work, such as rezoning a parcel of vacant land.

Another variation of capitalizing on the inaction of others
is to *invest where the person you are dealing with recognizes
the opportunity, but can't do anything about it.*

These investment opportunities are created where poorly
conceived properties, slow lease-ups, and unexpected financial demands outstrip the ability of owners to maintain
properties and pay the necessary carrying costs. In the single-
family home market, bargains may become available when a
divorce or transfer to another city forces a quick sale, denying
the owner the luxury of waiting for a buyer willing to pay
top dollar.

This form of investing may sound vaguely exploitative, but
it always takes place because the seller is *motivated*. If you
don't buy the property, someone else will.

The fact that a property has to be sold, even if it is losing
money, does not make it a bad property. *The goal is to find
distressed owners instead of distressed properties.* Often, it is
a question of the price one pays to acquire an investment.
With sufficient reserves allocated for completing a building
or weathering a weak rental market, a property which lost
money for its first owner may well make money for the next.

This is not a sure thing. Some properties are so poorly conceived they may never succeed. Others are conceptually
sound, but may never find their market.

Places to look for pockets of investment opportunity include:

1. *New property or product types.* Congregate-care facilities have proven their success in many cities and are very "in line" with demographic trends. So-called R&D facilities, which are industrial warehouses with a high percentage of finished office space and certain other modifications, may still be attractive development or conversion projects in some markets. Condominiumized boat slips or garage spaces are beginning to appear in some cities. Who knows?

2. *Overbuilt and distressed markets.* In one man's ruins may lie another man's fortune. Purchasing properties which are in distress or getting them on the courthouse steps can be a very profitable occupation if there is reason to expect ultimate recovery. Provide for sufficient reserves and don't be afraid to try to renegotiate debt. Remember that banks and S&Ls are watched by regulatory agencies and do not want to be in the real estate ownership business; they will go to great lengths to avoid moving a loan to the nonperforming column.

3. *Out-of-favor investments.* Regional shopping centers, office buildings, strip shopping centers, and new residential properties all have been in—and out—of favor. There are signs in the industry of increasing interest in industrial warehouses, townhouses, and possibly older, well-located office buildings. Every dog has its day.

4. *Ignored markets.* When a market is not in the spotlight, the initial yields on existing real estate tend to be greater than in the hot locations. This is because growth will supposedly be relatively flat. Just because the Rust Belt has fallen on hard times does not mean people don't live there and that some markets are not strong. Find the market which will be in the spotlight *tomorrow*, then invest *today*. Get high initial yield *and* steep growth.

5. *Strategic real estate.* Remember supply and demand. As obvious as this seems, there is a lot of "B" and "C" real estate in "A" locations that will only increase in value. Don't feel you have missed the boat just because prices are already starting up, and don't think the boat doesn't exist just because prices are low. "Columbus investing" often falls into this category. It can require courage and patience.

Using the market inefficiency in real estate to find above-market yields is just another refinement of the strategic planning level of the Common Sense Pyramid. Which form of market inefficiency you select to focus on will be a function of your own inclinations, skills, and resources.

Part II

Investing in Real Estate Yourself

CHAPTER 5

How to Buy Property

To Buy or Not to Buy

Part I, "Understanding Real Estate," introduced the basics of real estate and real estate investment, and showed how common sense and each person's own experience can be used to demystify real estate investment. The Common Sense Pyramid was provided as a means to develop expertise and go off in pursuit of properties; major concepts essential to grasping real estate dynamics were introduced; and market inefficiency was presented as a powerful means to *always* make low risk/high return property investments. What could be left?

Plenty.

Let us suppose you find a property. All the signs are right. It is an apartment building which has been allowed to run down. Demand for apartments is strong in your area. You will fix the steps, trim the hedges and maybe do a little landscaping, fix the plaster and put new appliances in the three vacant apartments, increase the rents, weed out the drug dealer and your unemployed brother-in-law when their leases come up for renewal, and petition the city for a reduction in your real estate taxes. All is right with the world.

Wait.

You can afford what the present owner is asking—which happens to be in line with what other buildings in the neighborhood have been sold for—but you would have nothing left for improvements to the building. Your unemployed brother-in-law pays his rent late, but at least he pays the rent. What good is another vacant apartment if it can't be fixed up to where it will be leasable?

A closer look at your figures shows that the other buildings which you are using as market comparables were all in better condition than this building. You can't go to the seller and just ask him to drop his price because you aren't sure how low you want him to drop it. You understand that even if the building (together with improvements) becomes affordable, it does not mean you are buying at the "right" price.

What is the right price?

To me, there are three aspects to the "right" price: (1) the right price *for you*; (2) the right price *for the seller*; and (3) the right price *for the property*. Only when all three aspects come together should a deal happen.

You have some sense of what you can afford, and the seller will ultimately let you know whether your offer is acceptable to him or her, so as a practical matter, your focus is on what a property is *worth*, and whether it will provide the financial return you require. Chapter 1 walked through the income statement and chapter 2 began to discuss this issue, pointing out that the return on investments should exceed one's alternative opportunities and compensate one for the risk being accepted. Neither, however, adequately discussed the proper way to *measure* return in real estate.

There are a number of techniques employed to measure return. Not all are appropriate in any given situation.

Initial cash-on-cash return and capitalization rates   Initial cash-on-cash return is probably the most common and popular way of expressing returns in real estate. You are considering buying a 10,000-square-foot warehouse. The entire building is leased on a triple-net basis (meaning, you will

recall, that all operating and maintenance expenses are paid
for by the tenant) for a ten-year term to Breakable Toy Company ("If it wobbles, it's Breakable!") for an annual rent of
$36,000. The seller's asking price is $300,000, comprised of
$100,000 cash and a $200,000 assumable mortgage. The loan
requires annual debt service of $34,000. The income state-
ment looks like this:

BREAKABLE TOY BUILDING
First-Year Income Statement

Rent	$36,000
Less: Expenses	0
Net Operating Income	36,000
Less: Debt Service	(34,000)
Net Cash Flow	$2,000

This is what you can expect for your first year—a $2,000 cash
return on a $100,000 cash investment: a 2-percent cash-on-
cash return.

This does not sound too good, but let us consider the seller's
asking price for a moment anyway. The *capitalization rate*
used by the seller is 2 percent. This means that the price was
set at the amount which would provide a buyer with a 2-
percent initial return. The price is calculated by dividing the
net cash flow by the capitalization rate (or "cap rate"), expressed in decimal rather than percentage form:

$$\frac{\text{Net Cash Flow}}{\text{Cap Rate}} = \text{Cash Purchase Price over Mortgage}$$

$$\frac{\$2,000}{0.02} = \$100,000$$

The property would also be described to be "capitalized at
2," or "capped at 2." If you are going to be active in the
world of real estate, it is good to understand its language.

If the property were being sold "free and clear"—that is,

with no mortgage—at the same price, the cap rate would be different. Net cash flow would be the same as net operating income; and instead of cash over mortgage we would simply insert the entire purchase price:

$$\frac{\$36,000}{\$300,000} = 0.12 \text{ or } 12\%$$

Notice the way in which the equation was rearranged:

$$\frac{\text{Net Cash Flow}}{\text{Purchase Price}} = \text{Cap Rate}$$

This is the way one calculates the cap-rate or cash-on-cash return being offered. Notice that cap-rate analysis generally does not include the value of first-year tax benefits to an investor, although this is also a valid number to calculate.

Cap rates are a simple concept, and are at the heart of real estate pricing: *What is the initial return on your investment?*

It should be obvious that a 2-percent return is far below what you could make on your money elsewhere. If the lease to Breakable Toy contained no rent increases for the entire ten-year term, we would surely want to negotiate for a better deal.

In our investigation of the marketplace, we would undoubtedly have determined the prevailing cap rates for comparable buildings, and we would try to bring our purchase price closer in line with those sales. Assuming, of course, that this would provide us with an attractive yield.

Overall yield and discounted cash-flow pricing   Obviously, the yield on an investment includes much more than what we make in a single year, whether that year is at the beginning or end of our expected holding period. This is particularly true of real estate, which tends to be a long-term investment with appreciating cash flow and value over time.

Changing cash flow is implicit in the way in which most properties operate. Renewal of leases at new rates reflecting market conditions at the time, and changes in the cost of insurance, maintenance, and other expenses serve to alter cash flow from one year to the next. Overall yield calculations and discounted cash-flow pricing are attempts to measure the effect of these future events on the current value of a property.

Take the example of a bond in Static E Phone Company. The bond costs $1,000, has a ten-year term, and pays $80 (8 percent) annually. At the end of the ten-year term, the bond is redeemed for $1,000. It has an 8-percent yield. Notice that the Static E bond also pays an 8-percent cash-on-cash return, and—although capitalization is not a concept applicable to corporate debt—in effect, reflects an 8-percent cap rate. This is true because where the cash dividend is constant and the residual value is equal to the original investment, cash-on-cash return and capitalization rate are equal to overall yield.

If the Breakable Toy lease provided for a level rent of $36,000 for the entire ten-year lease term, and if Breakable had an option to purchase the building for $100,000 over the loan balance (the same price at which it was purchased) at the end of the lease term, then the asking price for the warehouse would reflect a 2-percent overall yield—the same as the initial cash-on-cash return and cap rate. We would most certainly not buy the building at this price.

It is unlikely that a seller—even the most optimistic one—would propose such a low cap-rate price unless he or she had reason to think a property would enjoy escalating rents and appreciating value.

Let us assume the Breakable Toy building provides for these escalating rents in its lease:

> Article 5. *Annual Rent.* Annual rent shall be $36,000 during the first two years of this lease, increasing by $4,000 at that time and on each two-year anniversary thereafter.

In other words, the rents would look like this:

Year 1:	$36,000	Year 6:	$44,000
Year 2:	$36,000	Year 7:	$48,000
Year 3:	$40,000	Year 8:	$48,000
Year 4:	$40,000	Year 9:	$52,000
Year 5:	$44,000	Year 10:	$52,000

Since debt service would remain constant, the increase in cash flow would be even more dramatic:

Year	Cash Flow	Annual Return on Investment (%)
1	$ 2,000	2
2	$ 2,000	2
3	$ 6,000	6
4	$ 6,000	6
5	$10,000	10
6	$10,000	10
7	$14,000	14
8	$14,000	14
9	$18,000	18
10	$18,000	18

Even if Breakable Toy had an option to purchase the property for $100,000 plus the mortgage balances—in other words, with no appreciation—the overall yield on this investment must be greater than 2 percent.

This is where discounted cash-flow pricing comes into use.

Discounted cash-flow analysis—also called *present value analysis*—is based on the premise that the present value of a sum of money expected in the future is worth less than its face amount at the time of receipt. Therefore, we would rather have $100 today than $100 in the future, and we would pay an amount *less than $100* in order to secure the receipt of $100 in the future. This reflects the time value of money.

Money is capable of *earning* money over time. Therefore,

if we have $100 today, we can invest it and have more than $100 in the future. Even a savings account paying 5-percent annual interest would give us $105 one year from now.

If 5 percent is the best we believe we can earn on our money, it becomes our *discount rate*. It is the rate by which we measure the time value of money.

If we are offered $5,000 four years from now, and our discount rate is 5 percent, then we would be willing to pay $4,113.51 for that amount today. *The present value of $5,000 in four years at a 5-percent discount rate is $4,113.51.*

This is easy to prove:

Present	$4,113.51
	× 1.05
Year 1	4,319.19
	× 1.05
Year 2	4,535.15
	× 1.05
Year 3	4,761.90
	× 1.05
Year 4	5,000.00

While it is obviously easy to figure out the present value of a sum due only one year away

$$\left(\frac{\text{future value}}{1 + \text{discount rate}} = \text{present value} \right),$$

it would be difficult to vary rates, terms, and amounts on paper without the assistance of either published present value tables or—far preferable in these modern times—hand calculators. Relatively inexpensive (under $100) calculators can do extremely sophisticated financial analysis, including everything discussed on these pages. The best choices at this writing are probably either Hewlett-Packard's HP-12C or Texas Instruments' Business Analyst.

Let us return to the Breakable Toy building. Assuming the

scheduled rent increases and residual option price represent
our cash flow, the present value of the investment is the sum
of the present values of the cash flow in each year, discounted
at the appropriate discount rate. This rate should reflect what
we want to earn on our money given the level of risk being
taken.

A warehouse net lease is not a very risky type of investment,
but real estate is illiquid, so let us choose 10 percent as a good
discount rate:

BREAKABLE TOY COMPANY BUILDING
Discounted Cash Flow Analysis

Year	Cash Flow	Present Value at 10%
1	$ 2,000	$ 1,818
2	$ 2,000	1,653
3	$ 6,000	4,508
4	$ 6,000	4,098
5	$ 10,000	6,209
6	$ 10,000	5,645
7	$ 14,000	7,184
8	$ 14,000	6,531
9	$ 18,000	7,634
10	$ 18,000	6,940
10 (Option)	$100,000	38,554

Total Present Value: $90,774

The total present value of the Breakable Toy building at a
10-percent discount rate is $90,774 (this calculation can be
reached through just one series of entries using "net present
value" functions on the calculators mentioned earlier). This
means that we would have an overall pre-tax yield of 10 percent if we were to purchase the Breakable Toy building for
$90,774.

The seller's asking price of $100,000 suddenly does not ap-
pear so unreasonable. If our required investment yield was
under 10 percent, we might be willing to pay the asking price;
if we wanted at least a 10-percent yield, we would try to

negotiate the price to the appropriate level. If the residual value at year ten was not fixed by an option, we would capitalize cash flow in that year at some rate—perhaps 10 or 11 percent, resulting in a higher sale price—and the asking price might be downright cheap.

The benefit of overall yield and discounted cash-flow pricing is that it allows us to value the appreciation potential of a property and its overall value relative to our investment alternatives. It also gives us a precise means to negotiate price.

It should be clear that discounted cash-flow pricing is only as good as the projections you use. While you do not wish to be so conservative that the indicated price is obviously far below the fair market value and what the seller will be willing to accept, it still pays to err on the side of caution. The example of the Breakable Toy Company building did not include either tax benefits or costs (such as a tax on gains over the depreciable basis at sale), potential appreciation of the property if Breakable Toy had no purchase option, or *any* monies for repairs or improvements which may affect cash flow. Your own analyses should include these considerations.

Internal rates of return   Internal rates of return are a special kind of discounted cash-flow analysis. All of these analyses are basically equations, where we supply all the available information and solve for one variable. In net present value analysis, we solve for *present value*, or *price*. In internal rate of return (IRR) analysis, we solve for *interest rate* or *yield*. Therefore, in the Breakable Toy building example, the internal rate of return at the $100,000 asking price was 8.86 percent. This means that had we used 8.86 percent as our discount rate, the indicated present value for the property would have been approximately $100,000.

IRR is a very useful concept, but one has to be careful with it. IRRs can be very misleading where the rate of return is high. This is because the calculation assumes that money earned in cash flow is immediately reinvested at the same rate. Therefore, a 46-percent IRR assumes the individual can always earn 46 percent on his or her money. Not likely. The effect of this is to make good investments look unbelievable. One might very well prefer to invest money at 16 percent for ten years than 46 percent for one year, if only 10-percent investments were available afterward.

One solution is to use an *adjusted IRR*, where the calculations reinvest money at a specified discount rate. Another is to use IRRs in conjunction with other methods of calculating yield.

Inappropriate measures of return   There are many ways of measuring return and yield. Most are inappropriate or downright misleading. Some of them include *rent multiples*, which may be of use in establishing general market price levels, but which should not be used to justify a given purchase price; *average return on investment*, which ignores the present value of money; *total return ratio*, another measurement ignoring present value; and *net cash invested*, a useful concept before tax reform, but one which is now of little importance.

Which price is right?

Your analysis for every property should employ a combination of return and yield measurements. This is *not* a fishing trip to find the one number that finally justifies the seller's price. This is a system of checks and balances to help you pay an amount which both satisfies your criteria for return and is consistent with values prevailing in the marketplace. Table 4 tracks the history of real estate yields and cap rates from 1979 to the middle of 1986, comparing them with AA bond yields. Notice that the higher risk of real estate results in yields usually exceeding that for the bonds.

Table 4 provides information for real estate yields from a national market in "institutional investment-grade properties." The yields and cap rates for smaller properties tend to

TABLE 4

Real Estate Yield and Capitalization Rate Trends, 1979–1986

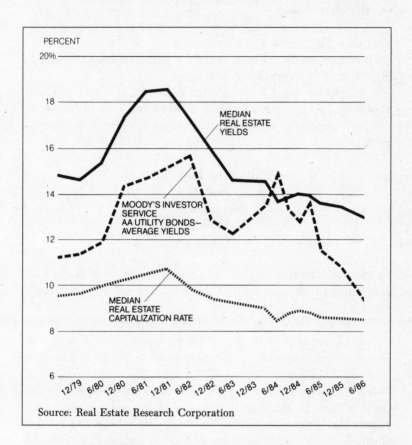

Source: Real Estate Research Corporation

be somewhat greater, and all measurements of return will vary from market to market. Yields and cap rates for all properties have risen somewhat since this table was compiled, reflecting the effect of tax reform and a perception of real estate as a somewhat riskier investment than it had been previously.

The price you pay for a property has a major impact on what you will ultimately earn on your investment. Any time

and effort you spend toward assessing that return and—
through informed negotiation—increasing it, will be well
worth your while.

Plighting Thy Troth

You have managed to negotiate a price. Where do you go
from there? A handshake? The bank?

It would be good to start with a handshake and you will
hopefully end up at the bank, but there are steps in between.

Every property acquisition contains certain key components:

Finding the Investment
Analysis
Negotiation
Due Diligence
Closing

These areas overlap in time and may vary in intensity at various parts of the acquisition process, but all are invariably
present.

There are two documents which usually appear in the
course of an acquisition: a letter of intent, and a contract.
The contract is obviously the culmination of the negotiation
process, dictating the terms of the acquisition at closing. The
letter of intent is a far more subtle document, serving a variety of uses in shaping the course of the acquisition. As a
buyer, the letter of intent is the means by which you protect
yourself in the acquisition process. It is imperative that you
understand its many uses.

You may wonder why you want protection.

The seller owns the real estate. He or she is under no obligation to be fair, reasonable, or ultimately to sell you the
property. The seller has little need for protection.

As a buyer, you are seeking an asset over which you have
no control or claim. You are trying to motivate another person to part with that claim on terms of your choosing. On the

way you must draw out information (and ascertain whether it is both accurate and complete), expend money on site visits and professionals, and probably put up a deposit in advance of closing. You are in very great need of protection.

Your initial conversations with the seller of the Breakable Toy building are somewhat informal. A sales package containing basic financial information was provided to you and a tour of the property was gladly arranged. Having come to the point where you feel confident that this is an asset you wish to acquire, the negotiations must become more formalized.

The owner has given you a summary of the lease, but is evasive whenever you request the entire document or loan materials. You are beginning to wonder whether the terms are as described and whether the property mortgage exists at all. In price discussions, the owner professes to be flexible, but will not commit himself. You feel like you are chasing your tail in pursuit of an unobtainable goal.

Enter the letter of intent.

Below is a sample letter of intent for the Breakable Toy building. You will notice that it accomplishes the following:

1. *A specific offer to purchase the property is conveyed to the seller.* Even if the proposal is not acceptable, the offer provides a focus for the seller's objections and continued negotiations.

2. *If the offer is accepted, the property is taken off the market.* Nobody wants to negotiate seriously for a property that is still up for grabs.

3. *Acceptance of the offer places a burden on the seller to provide information.* Notice that no down payment is due until contingencies are removed. These contingencies allow you to verify that the facts are as they were presented. Suddenly, the seller has a stake in cooperation and *you* have the

right to determine whether a contingency has been satisfied. A smart buyer will keep some measure of control in the contingency period and possibly require a down payment in advance (not unreasonable positions), but the letter of intent signifies a shift to serious "due diligence" and progress toward closing.

4. *The letter of intent creates a quasi-binding outline for a final closing.* There is both a schedule and a set of terms contained in the letter of intent. Major issues of price and possibly terms are set forth, but the document is still short of a contract. In theory, either party can still find a way out. The letter of intent will be of varying legal force from state to state and depending on how it is written (even if a document is *called* a letter of intent, at some point the language within can give it greater force, so a lawyer should almost certainly be involved in its drafting), but it is most important as a moral imperative to proceed in good faith.

LETTER OF INTENT
(Buyer's Letterhead)

October 19, 1987

J.Q. Breakable, President
Breakable Toy Company
World Headquarters Circle
Breakville, USA

Re: Breakable Toy Building
Industrial Park
Letter of Intent

Dear Mr. Breakable:

As I advised you in our meeting this morning, I am prepared to purchase the Breakable Toy Building, Industrial Park (the "Property"), subject to acceptance by you of the following terms and conditions:

1. The purchase price for the Property shall be Three Hundred Thousand ($300,000.00) Dollars, comprised of $100,000.00 cash and

assumption of the existing $200,000.00 mortgage from Dollar Bank of Breakville.

2. The existing ten-year triple-net lease to Breakable Toy Company shall be in effect at Closing.

3. The Breakable Toy lease shall be amended to modify the lessee purchase option for One Hundred Thousand ($100,000.00) Dollars plus mortgage balances up to the greater of (a) $100,000.00 plus mortgage balances, or (b) eighty-five (85%) percent of appraised value.

4. A cash deposit of $10,000.00 shall be paid into escrow within five (5) business days after release by Buyer of conditions and contingencies to this offer. This deposit shall be refundable only if the parties cannot agree on the terms of this contract.

5. No brokerage commission shall be payable by any party as a result of this transaction.

6. Closing shall take place within sixty (60) days after release by Buyer of the following conditions and contingencies, not to be unreasonably withheld:

(a) Seller will provide Buyer with all documents and records related to the Property within ten (10) days of acceptance of this offer. These documents shall include, but not be limited to, leases, architectural plans, mortgage, historical financial statements, books, appraisals, and surveys.

(b) Buyer and Buyer's agents shall have reasonable access to the Property for the purpose of property and engineering surveys and inspections.

(c) Buyer shall commission a title search for the Property, to be completed within thirty (30) days of acceptance of this offer, the cost of which shall be deducted from the purchase price at Closing.

(d) Buyer shall prepare the initial draft of the contract, to be provided within ten (10) business days after release by Buyer of all conditions and contingencies. Each party will bear its own legal costs.

(e) The contract must be mutually acceptable to both parties.

(f) Upon acceptance of this offer, Seller shall cease offering of

the Property, and any discussions with other parties regarding purchase of the Property.

(g) Both parties agree that time is of the essence.

This offer is valid until November 1, 1987, after which it shall be considered withdrawn.

If the terms and conditions of this offer are acceptable, please sign
where indicated below and return one (1) copy by certified mail.

Very truly yours,

(Buyer)

ACCEPTED AND AGREED TO:

By: _____
Date: _____

As you can see, the letter of intent gets things moving. It
separates the serious seller from those who would waste your
time and money, and it provides a schedule for moving toward closing. The specific form of the letter of intent will be
tailored to each property, depending on the situation, the level
of cooperation being given by the seller, and your own level
of interest.

Closing, when and if you reach it, is largely a ceremony
organized and conducted by lawyers to commemorate your
successful negotiation of a transaction and contract. Your sig-
nature will be required many times and—with luck—very
few items will need to be resolved at the last minute. Still,
for a closing to occur—and it *must* occur if you are to take
possession of a property—every single detail must be worked
out between you and the seller, and this is something which
should not be delegated to lawyers. The property and the
money are yours, not theirs.

Acquiring property is very much a courtship between you
and the seller of a property. Beware the tease who would take
your ring and leave you at the altar.

Kicking the Bricks

On my desk I keep a photograph of a large office building being demolished by implosion. Superimposed over the crumbling structure are the words: "We Kick the Bricks."

Hopefully, this will not be the result when you go out to inspect a prospective acquisition, but if crumble it must, crumble it shall. It is far better to know the problems with a property before you acquire it than to discover them after closing, when the problems and their attendant costs are yours to bear.

Kicking the bricks—also known simply as "due diligence"—is the exercise of prudence before plunging into an acquisition. It is exactly the same as checking out a used car, where the term obviously originates. While the needs of each due diligence will vary from property to property, the following checklist provides some of the major items:

- Engineer's inspection
- Title search to discover liens on property
- Review of leases and all major documents
- Review of historical financial statements
- Investigation to discover impending problems, such as departure of a major tenant

Finding a problem may not necessarily kill your deal. It may be possible to reduce the agreed-upon purchase price to allow the payment of liens on the property or to cover unexpected costs. You may also decide to have your lawyer insert broad representations by the seller into the contract, which will afford you some basis for protection should undisclosed costs or problems come to light later.

The most important thing is that no stone be left unturned in your search for potential problems. Allowing yourself to rush a purchase because a deal seems "too good to be true" may get you in trouble precisely because it *was* too good to be true.

Never get so attached to a transaction that you cannot kill

it before it kills you. This is not an easy thing to do since an inordinate amount of ego (and money) may be tied up in completing an acquisition. A builder who constructs a home and sells it at a loss can point to the structure and take credit for it; nobody will ever know of his mistakes. No such consolation exists for the property acquisition that falls through. There is nothing to show for your efforts.

This is the wrong attitude. It is far better to walk away from a bad deal than to go through with it out of a misplaced sense of accomplishment. All you will really accomplish is to lose money.

There is always another deal.

CHAPTER 6

How to Own Property

When the Seller Drives Away

When the due diligence is done, the mortgage in place, the closing concluded, and you watch the seller driving away in his new Mercedes, it is just the beginning of the Great Real Estate Adventure.

The projections you have so carefully crafted from weeks, perhaps months, of market research and property inspections are just that—*projections*. Something—or many things—must be done to bring them into reality.

If you are lucky, the property will be net leased to a single tenant—such as Breakable Toy—or fully leased up. If it is a shopping center, office building, or industrial structure, the nearest lease expiration date for a tenant may be some distance in the future.

More often, this is not the case. In truth, you probably do not *want* this to be the case.

If you have gathered anything from the preceding chapters, it is probably that the best opportunities for profit in real estate are where properties are not being managed to realize their full potential. You will therefore want to prepare a business plan indicating which tenants you intend to keep and who will go when their leases are up, what physical changes need to be made, where operating efficiencies can be achieved, and how you will go about filling vacant space. The rent roll and income statements used in your acquisition campaign are your first and best planning tools.

While you are doing this, there are other items which must be attended to on a day-to-day basis. Some of the major issues which must be addressed include:

- *Debt service before self-service.* If you don't pay the mortgage, it means foreclosure. Plenty of time later to line your pockets.
- *Set aside reserves for future capital improvements.* It is not a question of whether the time will come for big repairs, but *when.* Depending on the condition and age of the real estate, set aside 3 to 5 percent of revenues every year. Hopefully, a significant amount was allocated for reserves when the property was purchased.
- *Negotiate new leases with your tenants well before the lease has expired.* A tenant without a lease either moves out, leaving you with *no* rent, or pays his or her old rent on a month-to-month basis, leaving you with less rent than you might otherwise receive. Negotiation takes time, as there may be many items to agree on. Six months prior to lease end is not too soon to start.
- *Preventive action is cheaper than delay.* There are few cases where deferred maintenance or Band-Aids are less expensive in the long run than addressing problems decisively when they arise. John Wayne would bite the bullet. So should you.

There is nothing about running a property at its full potential that cannot be accomplished through hard work, attention to detail, and constant vigilance.

Love is blind. Don't you be. It is easy to fall in love with your real estate and to see it as something it is not. Few properties are suitable for high-fashion boutiques or the most prestigious law firms. Those that are may not necessarily be more profitable than what you own. A property is what it is. As philosophical as this sounds, it is a very important thing to remember.

Owning real estate is not easy. Perhaps that is why it can pay so handsomely.

Properties Do Not Run Themselves

You must either see to it that floors are swept, garbage is removed, and repairs are made, or be prepared to do it yourself. The same applies to collecting rents and paying bills. A property cannot be allowed to slide. It is a business and, like any venture, will lose its customers (e.g., tenants) if it is poorly run.

For many the solution is to hire an outside management company. There are groups which specialize in the operation of various types of property, generally charging fees ranging from 3 to 6 percent of gross rental revenues. The proper fee will vary from market to market. Do research on management companies just as you checked out the market for real estate. Look for people with good references, a solid organization, and experience in operating your type of property. A few good national firms exist, but local management tends to be better. Be sure your manager provides an annual operating budget. If you know who your manager will be, it is best to involve him or her before you even close on the acquisition. It is very common for a buyer to make optimistic projections, only to have the management company come in and inform him or her that the numbers are unrealistic and cannot be achieved.

If you need to lease up a considerable amount of space, you may wish to structure an incentive fee; nobody wants to pay more than they have to for management, but you are doing yourself a disservice if you fail to adequately motivate your manager. Also, beware of the management company which owns a property in direct competition with your own. It is not difficult to figure out whose property will lease up first and get the best tenants.

The list of considerations is literally endless. Let common sense be your guide.

How to Become a Seller

If you have been a buyer (and you probably have if you own a property), then you may have some idea of what it takes to be an effective seller.

Being an effective seller entails walking a fine line between pushover and monster. While you do not want to be easy on terms and accommodating in every respect, neither should you be so unyielding and difficult that a buyer is never drawn into negotiations and a sale is never made. Always remember that the goal is to sell your property at an acceptable price.

The resulting strategy is one part terms and nine parts psychology. First let us examine terms.

Setting a price. The first step in setting a price for your property is to know what it is worth. Approach your property as if you were a buyer. Prepare projections, do a study of comparable sales in the area. You may possibly commission an appraisal, even if you ultimately choose not to use it. Try to assess the trend of the market. In a rising market, someone has to lead prices upward. It may as well be you. In a falling market, prices must reverse at some level. Again, it may as well be you. When you finally set your price, err well on the high side. Put your property in its best possible light, then add 20 to 30 percent to the resulting number. (When I sell my own properties to readers of this book, I will clearly have to add more!)

What do you need? The price you will ultimately get for your property will not necessarily reflect your hopes for the investment, but you should know what you are willing to accept. Try to determine the *fair* price for your property, and refuse to go below that level. Use your attorney, accountant, and other trusted advisers as objective sources of opinion and to hone your strategies. Know how quickly you must sell your property, and how long you are willing to wait for your money. Be aware of tax ramifications from your sale.

What will you do? Know in advance whether you will take back a mortgage on part of the sale price, and at what interest rate. Is the approval of new zoning an acceptable contingency? Is a tax-free exchange for another property of interest to you? Would you consider retaining a piece of the equity? Would you split a parcel of land or a group of buildings? These are things best left unsaid until negotiations are underway, but it is important that you know the answers should the buyer suggest these possibilities or if you see these techniques as a means to get what you want.

From there on, the business of selling your property is marketing. You have a product, and you want to sell it at the highest price possible.

Finding buyers. A real estate broker is probably the best means of putting a property on the market. It will reach the widest audience of buyers and, if you don't like the price after the broker's commission has been factored in, you don't have to sell. Shop around for a good broker. Get recommendations. When you pick one, stick with him or her. Try to avoid signing an exclusive (although this isn't always possible), for if they fail to perform, there is no reason to be stuck. Agree on initial offering terms and on the commission in advance. Be sure the broker is working for *you*, but remember that your interests will not necessarily be the same. Make it clear that you must approve the selling package. Also—and this is very important—*do not allow your property to be offered indiscriminately* in a mass mailing. Nothing kills buyer interest faster than a property which has been "shopped."

The offering package. A good offering package will be crisp, to the point, and professional. If the offering package is high quality, there will be a presumption that your property is high quality. If the package is sloppy, it will rub off on your investment. I would recommend dropping any broker suggesting a "cut and paste" offering package. The offering should include a description of the property, picture, site plan, price (but not detailed terms), financing summary if relevant, rent roll, and pro forma income statement. If the buyer has any interest, there will be plenty of time later to provide and work out details.

Projections. If you believe in your property, it is always tempting to provide projections showing its staggering potential. This can be tricky. On the one hand, you do not want to prevent a buyer from coming up with more favorable projections than your own numbers would provide. On the other hand, outrageously aggressive projections only undermine the credibility of your offering. Projections are useful if they are not too detailed and if they illuminate some aspect of a property's potential which would otherwise be missed, such as the renewal of leases currently at below-market rent rates. Most of the time you are best off holding back numbers until they can aid you in negotiations. You would rarely lead with your trump card in bridge; don't do it in a game with higher stakes.

Presenting your property. One of the first things a prospective buyer will do is to visit your property. If you have the opportunity to lead the tour, you will want to take the buyer on a tour of the neighborhood, showing competitive properties and placing your property in the context of the overall marketplace. As you approach the property, use the route with the nicest homes and shopping, and the best site visibility. You have an opportunity to set first impressions and it should not be wasted. In any event, your property should be especially well maintained and clean during the period in which you are offering it. During this very early stage of courtship, you and your property should be "friendly" and accessible. As the seller becomes more interested and commits more time to the acquisition process, he or she will find it harder to withdraw.

Negotiations. Everything is negotiable, *at a price.* Always bear this in mind. If you set up barriers to doing business with inflexible requirements, you will soon be alone again with your property. This does not mean that you should encourage a buyer who is clearly unwilling or incapable of meeting your price. It means that reasonable queries deserve reasonable responses.

Keeping control. At the heart of the negotiation process is the knowledge by both parties that the seller has something the buyer wants. The buyer has money, of course, but so do other people; only you have your property. This forms the basis for keeping control of the sale. Do not appear anxious to sell, even if you are. It will only harden the buyer's position. Be decisive, even when you do not feel it. If you need time to make a response, take the time; when you finally give your answer, state it firmly and without vacillation. Being fair in negotiations does not weaken this position. If you are negotiating seriously with one party, reveal this to other prospective buyers. Once you sign a letter of intent and deposit monies have been placed in escrow (or given on a nonrefundable basis if you can get it), pull the property off the market.

Due diligence. I have always thought it particularly responsible and professional for a seller to have all necessary documents neatly assembled in advance for a buyer in the due-diligence phase. After all, the seller is aware that this phase will eventually be reached; there is no reason this simple courtesy should not be extended. At this stage, the seller must maintain a delicate balance between the desire to withhold negative information about his or her property and the need to avoid misrepresentations. Given a difficult choice, avoid misrepresentations. You need not volunteer everything you know, but a deliberate misstatement or violation of contract terms forms the basis for a virtually certain lawsuit and/or the loss of a time-consuming sale.

Getting tough. Some buyers will attempt to change terms or negotiate price in the final phases of a sale, possibly at closing itself (as will some sellers). If a genuinely significant new fact has not emerged, they are probably relying on the previously mentioned tendency for parties to become committed to a sale as they invest more time in it. In their panic to save the sale, they agree to things that would not be acceptable at the outset. This is a particularly loathsome (but effective) technique. *Be tough.* The buyer has invested as much time and money in the sale as you have, and will be unwilling to see things fall apart unless he or she was never serious in the first place. The reaction of some people to this tactic is to withdraw completely "on principle." I do not recommend this either. If minor concessions can allow all parties to save face, then this is not so bad. But remember, at the outset you determined the limits of what you needed from the sale and what you were willing to do; there is nothing about another party's last-minute demands that changes these needs, unless you let them.

Closing. Little things always come up at closing. Handle them calmly and precisely, making sure that nothing jeopardizes the arrangements you have carefully shepherded to this point. If you have been skillful, you should walk away from the lawyer's offices with a check meeting or exceeding your original goals.

Some people have trouble with the morality of selling a property for more than it is worth. This is utter nonsense. Your responsibility as a seller is to get as much as you can for your property without passing it off as something which it is not. As discussed in chapter 4, it is the inefficiency of the market which makes real estate a truly superior investment. In part, this means there is money to be made by buying from unsophisticated sellers and selling to unsophisticated buyers. You only need one buyer who is willing to pay your price.

Selling is crucial because it is here that real estate appreciation is realized. Properties can be bought on the strength of wonderful projections, but if they fail to produce the expected cash flow and increase in value, then your investment will be disappointing. That is not an acceptable outcome.

CHAPTER 7

A Borrower and a Lender Be

When to Borrow

One of the most famous lines ever written by William Shakespeare is "Neither a borrower nor a lender be." The admonition is not correct. *Hamlet*, the play from which the line comes, was, after all, a tragedy.

A basic understanding of debt is essential to understanding real estate. Entire books are written just on the subject of real estate financing, but a relatively short discussion can illuminate some major facets of borrowing.

Basically, borrowing money to reduce the amount of equity capital required to buy a property—also called *leveraging*, because it levers the power of equity—is a means by which risk and return are increased in real estate. Positive leverage, where the interest rate on a mortgage is below the rate of return from a property, amplifies cash-on-cash yields. Negative leverage, where interest rates exceeded returns, has the effect of diminishing current yield. Negative leverage is clearly the less desirable situation, but interest rates are not a function of choice. You take what you can get. In either case, leverage makes the impact of appreciation more dynamic than would otherwise be the case.

Table 5 compares the effects of buying a shopping center

TABLE 5

PURCHASE OF $1 MILLION SHOPPING CENTER

A. *Financial Projections*		
Purchase Price	$1,000,000	
Net Operating Income Before Debt Service		
Year 1	80,000	
Year 2	100,000	
Year 3	120,000	
Year 4	140,000	
Year 5	160,000	
Sale Price (Year 5)	2,000,000	
B. *Potential Loan*		
Maximum Loan Available at 10% Interest	$800,000	
Annual Debt Service	80,000	
C. *Return Comparison*	*All Cash Buyer*	*Buyer Using Debt*
Cash Outlay	$1,000,000	$200,000
Initial Cash-On-Cash Return	8%	0%
Year 5 Return	16%	40%
Profit on Sale	$1,000,000	$800,000
Overall Pre-tax Yield	23.7%	40.6%

for all cash with the returns to a buyer borrowing 80 percent of the purchase price. In this case—showing negative leverage—initial cash-on-cash return is reduced from 8 percent to zero, but appreciating cash flow quickly makes the leveraged situation more attractive in both current return and overall yield.

This takes us to the heart of the leverage question: When should one borrow?

On the one hand, we can argue that mortgage debt is appropriate wherever it enhances yield. The other position would be that while the yield may be enhanced, the overall amount of money being earned is smaller, and that borrowing therefore makes no sense if the investor has other funds he or she cannot place at equally advantageous yields. As for increased risk, borrowing raises the break-even threshold (remember chapter 1) for a property—thus exposing one to the increased likelihood of foreclosure—but the overall size of the investment at risk is much less (presuming one is dealing with nonrecourse debt).

The argument over *how much* debt should be placed on a property has been made more acute since tax reform. In the past, one effect of borrowing was to increase tax benefits, since depreciation remains the same regardless of equity investment. In the wake of tax reform, leverage levels dropped as investors sought to eliminate unneeded tax benefits. This was particularly true in the syndication industry as sponsors attempted to entice investors with higher initial yields.

Reducing leverage is not necessarily appropriate for the direct buyer of real estate, whose primary goal has always been, and shall remain, high overall yield rather than tax shelter.

Table 6 explores the situations calling for various levels of debt. Few properties or investors will have all the hallmarks of one leverage scenario, but the table provides some guidelines to use as a starting point. In practice, a blend of conditions and personal goals will dictate. As always, one will be limited by the mortgages actually available from various sources.

Let us consider the components and terms of those mortgages.

The Anatomy of a Mortgage

A large part of understanding debt is understanding the parts that together comprise a mortgage. We are concerned here only with *nonrecourse* mortgages, which are based on the value of a property rather than the credit and net worth of the borrower. If a borrower fails to repay a recourse mortgage, a lender may look to the borrower's other assets; in a nonrecourse mortgage default, the property—whatever its worth may be—is the only security for the loan.

TABLE 6

HOW MUCH DEBT IS THE RIGHT DEBT?

Debt Level	Conditions
High 70–100%	Low interest rates Interest rates below property return Other high-yield investment opportunities Buyer has net passive *income* in existing portfolio Low-risk property Little need for current income
Medium 40–70%	Balanced passive income basket Moderate conditions in other categories
Little or No 0–40%	High interest rates Interest rates above property return Few other attractive investments available Net passive *losses* in portfolio High-risk property Need for high current income

Most people are at least generally familiar with borrowing through their experiences with their home mortgage. Certain components are present in almost all mortgages:

Principal: The amount borrowed (and owed).

Interest rate: The percentage rate paid for the use of the lender's money. Usually calculated and paid monthly in advance, but more favorable quarterly or annually in arrears (the end of the period).

Term: The length of time for which a loan is made.

Amortization:	Payments of principal made during the term of the loan. Calculated so that a loan fully amortizes (is completely repaid) over a certain period, usually the term but sometimes a longer period.
Debt service:	The total of interest and amortization payments made in a given period.
Security:	The property or assets pledged to the lender to cover the repayment of loan principal in the event debt service is not paid.

Commercial lending has its own world of special demands apart from residential mortgages. Larger amounts of money, higher risks, and loan security that is expected to cover its own debt service have resulted in new types of loans, devices to protect lenders, and accommodations for the unique needs of different owners and properties.

Some of the most common such features include:

Balloon payments:	Unpaid principal due at the end of the term, usually when a loan was interest-only or when the period for amortization exceeds the term of the loan.
Restrictive covenants:	Restrictions imposed by the lender, generally on matters such as transferability or assignment of the mortgage on sale of the property. Also prohibitions on taking out subordinated debt or second mortgages.
Financial covenants:	Requirements that the property maintain specified levels of reserves or that the borrower maintain a certain net worth. Not very common.
Points:	Various fees paid upon commitment of a mortgage. Sometimes for making the loan; sometimes a means of "buying down" the interest rate.

Accruals:	Used as a means of securing high loan-to-value ratio loans, a portion of interest which is not payable at the time it is incurred. Dangerous because it gives the impression that a property is breaking even or making money when this may not be the case.
Variability:	Interest rates which are variable, moving in accordance with some index in the economy such as the prime rate. Can be very favorable when governed by floors and ceilings, or where a higher pay rate builds a reserve for future increases in interest rates.
Participation:	Lender participation in net operating income or value above specified levels, usually given in exchange for a lower base interest rate.

This is far from an exhaustive list of loan features, but it gives some sense of how mortgages function and the flexibility that is available in some sectors of the debt markets.

How to Get into Debt

Sources for financing vary depending on who you are, the type of property you are trying to borrow against, and whether you require—or want—some special form of debt. Also, the availability of money may be a function of economic conditions beyond your control.

Places to start are your own bank (any relationships you already have offer the greatest possibility of expeditious financing), mortgage brokers, banks, and savings and loans in the area where the property is located, and the seller of the property.

Your own bank. If you have a good credit rating, this is almost always the best bet for the mortgage you want. These are people who know you and can easily verify your credit and business background. Hopefully, your bank will cherish its relationship with you and want to continue and enlarge the business you do with them. Take note that we are still talking about nonrecourse debt. *Anyone* can get a recourse loan if they have the net worth to back it up; your bank is doing you no favor if that is the best they can offer. Generally, your chances of special consideration are in inverse relationship to the size of the bank. At big banks, you mean little to them; at little banks, every customer is big. If you have been a good customer, you shouldn't *need* special consideration.

Mortgage brokers. Mortgage brokers don't make loans, but they know where to find them. For a few percentage points in fees (discuss fees ahead of time, since they may be negotiable), they will find you a loan. It isn't nice to use *every* mortgage broker in town, but there is nothing wrong with using a few. Ask your bank or people with similar properties for recommendations to the best. Mortgage brokers also have best access to taxable bonds and any government loan programs which may exist for the type of investment you want to make. Not too many of these programs still exist, but it never hurts to ask. When you do finally get your loan, if it is a little more expensive than you were led to expect or than you can afford, don't be afraid to go back to try to beat down that fee again.

Local financial institutions. Bankers love to watch their money. That is why banks and savings and loans favor investments in their own communities. It is easier to spot trouble before it is too late, and the institution can truthfully claim to be putting money back into the local economy. If you believe in "trickle-down" economics, that eventually means more deposits for the bank. Another advantage of going with the locals is that they provide an objective, informed opinion on your project. If they don't want to loan money against a local property, ask yourself (and them) *why.*

The seller. It pays to take note of this last source. The Tax Reform Bill of 1986 extended the at-risk rules to real estate where mortgages are not from a third party. The seller is *not* such a third party. This means that you cannot take deductions in excess of your own equity investment in a property if you are using seller financing, a change made to prevent abusive mark-ups of selling prices for the sole purpose of creating tax benefits. With the reduced tax benefits in real estate, this is of little consequence. Your main reason for borrowing should be to enhance your returns. If seller financing reduces your equity investment and makes an investment more affordable, you should definitely avail yourself of it. Seller financing generally offers better terms than outside debt, and is a fast, easy source of capital in acquisitions where it can be negotiated. Do *not* use seller financing as a means of overpaying for a property which is not worth it.

Where the Grass is Greener

Suppose you wanted to become a lender.

It is a capital-intensive business requiring a great deal of money. A secondary-mortgage market exists, but probably not for the type of loan you would be able to make, so there is really no liquidity. You have no control whatsoever over the management of the property to which you are lending. You probably do not have enough money to lend to get into a diversified pool of mortgages, so your risk is concentrated. Finally, if you have to foreclose, it is likely to be an extensive, pitched legal battle which will end with a settlement netting you only a partial return on your investment.

If this is still something you want to do, you may at least take comfort in the knowledge that you can have a lien on the property to which you are lending; you may be able to negotiate recourse to the borrower's overall net worth; the loan you are likely to make will provide a premium interest level (i.e., for junior debt, small properties, special types of real estate); the term might not be long, if this is a "bridge" situation; and nobody wants to be driven into bankruptcy, so the chances are good the borrower has ample motivation to repay you.

Finally, a good supply of loan prospects is also difficult to find. Possible sources include leaving your name and requirements with mortgage bankers and brokers, advertising, and, if you are sufficiently familiar with the market, offering your money only where you know the need exists.

An easier and safer way to lend is to invest in one of the many real estate mortgage funds or debt securities. These have lower yields than you could get as a direct lender, but returns are probably better than rated bonds. Also, many of the funds are listed on the stock market, providing some measure of liquidity.

If you do decide to lend money directly, the best advice is to negotiate ruthlessly. If the borrower was in a great position, the chances are good that he or she would go to a bank instead of to you. Things you should try to do include:

- Keep the value to loan ratio low; 1.5:1 is good, verified by an appraisal.
- Keep the debt-service coverage ratio high; 1.5:1 is again a good number, verified by established performance as seen in leases and certified financial statements.
- Insist on recourse or partial recourse to the borrower. Even covering the last ten to twenty cents on your dollar significantly increases your security and probably does not jeopardize the borrower's tax situation.
- Keep the term short. It usually takes time for a property to go bad. The shorter the term of the loan, the more likely a situation can be kept under control. You can always extend or reloan the money if all is well. Also, it is less likely that interest rates will move against you.
- Do not allow accruals. Whatever the rate is on your loan, that should be the pay rate. Accruals mask an inability to pay and erode value-to-loan ratio.
- Stay local. If this practice is good enough for banks, it is good enough for you. It is important to be able to monitor your investment.

- Look for distressed owners, not distressed properties. This is the same recommendation given for acquisitions. Look for someone who can't get a loan due to lack of time, not because the property is bad. Do your own due diligence to determine the problem; don't accept the prospective borrower's explanation for his or her troubles at face value.
- Get an interest-rate premium. Get 2 to 3 percent above the going rate for first mortgages, 4 to 6 percent for second mortgages. This is a premium over a bank's current real estate loan rate, not over prime.

Few people are going to take such a loan. That is just fine. Don't let your negotiating stand crumble—you only need a few good-quality loans on your terms. Do lots of due diligence and, when all else fails, err on the conservative side by saying *no*.

The final and most important rule is: *Loan only to properties you would be willing to own and operate.* The Law of Implied Willingness suggests that if you are willing to loan, you must be willing to foreclose, and therefore to own. Don't think it can't happen to you. It can. If you provide mortgages only to properties which you would happily own with no loss of sleep, then you will never get burned in the business of lending.

Part III

Investing in Real Estate Through Others

CHAPTER 8

When Others
Do the Buying

Something for Everybody

Buying real estate yourself is not for everyone.

Do not despair. If you lack the time or inclination (no one needs lack the *ability*) to find and acquire your own properties, alternatives do exist. As a matter of fact, having others do the buying offers sufficient advantages to going it alone that many real estate professionals—including myself—sometimes invest in deals put together by others in addition to their own investments.

An entire marketplace—the real estate syndication industry—is dedicated to the creation and sale of real estate investment opportunities for those who do not wish to get involved with the day-to-day hassle of property acquisition and management. The real estate syndication industry was developed on the strength of tax shelters in the decade preceding tax reform, but it involves far more. Real estate syndications offer a veritable smorgasbord of investment alternatives.

Properties come in every size, shape, and type imaginable, packaged for investors with anywhere from $1,000 to $1 million to spend. Some of the major types of offerings include:

Raw land speculation
Development/new construction

Existing real estate
Rehabilitation
Mortgage or participating mortgage pools

As you can see, the categories span the course of the property life cycle, as well as both the equity and debt side of transactions. In addition, all types of property in all parts of the country are syndicated at some time or another. In theory, there is no investment scenario which could not eventually be found in syndication form, although as a practical matter it may be hard to find a particular combination of property type, location, and investment program in affordable form at the time you wish to invest.

Few people would (or should) be determined to find such a specific situation. Whether or not to invest in a deal should be determined by how well it stacks up in each of four areas: real estate; sponsor; terms (structure); and need. These seem like very basic areas, but it is important to understand the essential relationship between these categories. Let us pose these standards as questions:

1. *Real estate:* Is the real estate opportunity attractive?
2. *Sponsor:* Can the sponsor make the most of the opportunity?
3. *Terms:* Do the terms of the deal allow you to see the benefits of what the sponsor produces?
4. *Need:* Are the benefits what *you* need and can afford?

Notice how each builds on the next. It is not enough that an investment pass muster in one, two, or even three of the areas—*it must make the grade in all four tests.* Think of the areas as steel vaults of increasing size, with each safe containing a smaller safe. The real estate itself, imprisoned in the smallest vault, is the jewel you are after, for it is the only asset of any value. However, if you are unable to unlock the boxes which encase it, its worth to you is greatly diminished.

Remember: *There is a good deal of great real estate, but*

only a few great deals. Your challenge as an investor is to find those few great deals, and never settle for anything less.

When Limited Partnerships Make Sense

The main means by which real estate is syndicated is through *limited partnerships.* A limited partnership is a form of ownership which provides distinct advantages over other organizational vehicles—say, corporations, sole proprietorships, or general partnerships—for real estate investment.

A limited partnership is comprised of a *general partner* and *limited partners.* The role of the general partner (usually one entity, but possibly several) is to organize the partnership, assemble or arrange for the assemblage of capital, manage the partnership (as distinct from the *property*, which the general partner or an affiliate may or may not manage), keep records, and make reports to the limited partners. The general partner is the *sponsor* of the investment and has liability for actions taken on behalf of the partnership.

Limited partners are basically *investors* purchasing *units* (shares) in a partnership. In most limited partnerships, the limited partners provide the bulk of equity capital, have no voice in management except under the most extraordinary conditions (and even then with difficulty), and in return *have no liability for the debts or actions of the partnership.* Given this description, it is no wonder that the Tax Reform Bill of 1986 specifically designates limited partners automatically to be *passive* participants in an activity. It is your investment as a limited partner with which we are interested in this chapter.

Major advantages of limited partnerships include:

Flow-through of income and expenses. Limited partnerships do not pay taxes as entities; taxable income and losses pass through to partners who are taxed as individuals as though they own the partnership's assets directly. For this reason, limited partnerships are often called "direct participation investments."

Diversification of financial risk. Most limited partnerships have many limited partners, each owning a small share of the partnership. The accumulated capital of these shares gives the partnership more flexibility and buying power than a single individual would have. Risk is therefore spread among many investors, and—in partnerships which acquire a portfolio of properties—spread among many assets.

Professional management. The combined capital of investors allows the partnership to hire professional management. Where management is also the sponsor, presumably the limited partners are attracted to the partnership partially because of management expertise.

Limited liability. Unless the terms of a partnership (to which investors have access in advance) specifically require one to put up additional capital, the liability of a limited partner cannot exceed his or her investment in the partnership. Combined with the ability to pass through income and losses without double taxation, this forms the basis for the appeal of the limited partnership format.

Limited partnerships are not without their disadvantages. There are two major ones:

Limited marketability. Unlike the stock market, except in rare circumstances, no ready market exists for limited partnership units. Even where sponsors provide mechanisms to repurchase units, there are usually conditions and limitations which serve to make the feature of little consequence in the situation which would make selling most attractive—trouble. With the exceptions to be discussed, limited partnerships—like real estate itself—should be considered illiquid investments.

Lack of management control. In the ordinary course of events, limited partners have no say in property or partnership management. In extraordinary circumstances (i.e., fraud, extreme mismanagement) it might be possible to get management control after lawsuits and great travail, *but it may well be at the cost of one's limited liability*. The government intended limited partners to have only limited rights. If you don't like it, don't invest.

Two other items bear mention as an advantage and a disadvantage, respectively, of limited partnership investment. These are tax incentives on the plus side, and the potential for further changes in the Tax Code on the negative side. These don't really have anything to do with the limited partnership vehicle itself.

Tax benefits—or lack thereof—arise from the nature of real estate or other investment categories. Because of the pass-through characteristic of limited partnerships, these vehicles have become a popular means of holding so-called "tax-advantaged" investment such as real estate. Still, one should not confuse the *conduit* for benefits with their *source*.

As for the risk that changes in the Tax Code may adversely affect investments, the Tax Reform Bill of 1986 was that nightmare come to life. However, this had nothing to do with limited partnerships *per se*. The 1986 legislation affects real estate in whatever form it is held. The next bill (there is *always* another bill) may change the rules for limited partnerships, real estate investment trusts, or corporations. Change in the Tax Code is surely an investment risk, but it is one which is hard to avoid. As always, the best course is to emphasize economically sound investments and hope for the best.

To prevent abuse, the special tax status accorded limited partnerships was granted by Congress subject to certain conditions regarding the financial *suitability* of investors. As a result of these suitability standards, partnership offerings fall into one of two categories: *public* or *private* offerings.

Public offerings are registered with the Federal Securities and Exchange Commission (SEC), which ensures that a deal meets certain standards of disclosure and reasonability (the SEC does not pass on the quality or investment merit of a program). As a result of this registration process (public limited partnerships are also called registered offerings), the sponsor may admit a virtually unlimited number of limited partners over the course of the offering period (usually one year) or until the full amount of capital specified in the offering has been raised, whichever comes first. The suitability standards for public offerings are modest, usually requiring that investors have net worth or income which would place them in the middle class, with minimum investment levels of only $1,000 or $2,000. It is estimated that $8 billion in capital was raised for real estate public offerings in 1985, 74 percent of the money raised for all registered partnerships.

The prospectus for the partnership—which contains relevant information about the offering, such as fees and deal terms—also indicates the type of investments which the partnership intends to make. Because of the large size of most real estate public offerings, which often raise tens and even hundreds of millions of dollars, the investment programs often involve acquisition of whole portfolios of properties.

Where these properties are known in advance, the offering is said to be *specified*; where a pool of money is being placed at the disposal of the sponsor, an offering is *unspecified*. Obviously, investing in an unspecified portfolio involves even greater reliance on a general partner/sponsor than would be the case if assets were known in advance. In addition to whether an offering is specified or unspecified, the prospectus will reveal the nature of the debt or equity positions being sought by the partnership, types of property, geographical areas, diversification requirements (if any), likely leverage ratios, and the overall investment objectives of the partnership (i.e., preservation of capital, appreciation, degree of tax shelter).

The prospectus also describes the major parties in an offering and provides the track record (past performance) of a general partner in prior partnership offerings. This is very important information which will be discussed in greater detail later in this chapter.

Private offerings are the second type of limited partnership programs. These investments rely on exemption from SEC registration under rules set forth in Regulation D of the Securities Act of 1933. As a result, private limited partnerships are often called "Reg D" offerings. The main thrust of these rules is stricter investor suitability standards, requiring (1) that investors be able to assess the risks and rewards of an investment, and (2) that all but thirty-five investors must be "accredited." The main definition of an accredited investor is that he or she must have a net worth (not including home, furnishings, or cars) in excess of $1 million. There are other means to be considered accredited, but this is the main definition.

Most investors in private offerings fall in with the thirty-five "nonaccredited" investor allowance. Even these investors must meet strict income and net worth suitability standards, which vary from offering to offering, but always require an ability to understand the risks associated with an investment.

Investors with the requisite income can satisfy the risk comprehension standards by hiring a lawyer or accountant to advise them. Due to the complexity and tax implications of most private partnership offerings, *it is almost always advisable to enlist professional assistance.* It would be difficult for me to overemphasize this last point. The amount of money involved is too great to do otherwise.

Ah. What *is* the amount of money involved?

Since Reg D offerings generally have far fewer investors than public partnerships, usually from ten to several hundred people, they raise larger amounts of money from each investor. The private deals we offer at my stockbrokerage firm generally involve limited partnership units costing from $50,000 to $150,000. Fractional units may be available, and many private deals are "staged-pay," meaning that the investment may be spread over several years with the unpaid portion secured by investor promissory notes; but this is still a very significant piece of change.

Prospectuses for private deals—also called "offering memorandums"—generally contain the same information found in those for public deals. However, due to the reduced scrutiny accorded to private investments, prospectus quality may vary considerably. Just because a memorandum has slick graphics on the cover, do not assume it fully or accurately discloses the risks of a given investment or that it is a good deal. By the same token, I have seen excellent deals in very plain wrappers. Once again, it is imperative that one engage professional assistance. Investing in a limited partnership goes far beyond the quality of the underlying real estate opportunity.

Although it does not pay to generalize, the quality of the real estate and sponsors involved in private deals—like the quality of the prospectuses—will tend to vary much more than for public offerings. I would expect to find the best and the worst investment opportunities in the private arena. This should really come as no surprise: Sponsors with the best deals know they can find investors and prefer not to bother with the costly, time-consuming process of SEC registration for any but the largest of projects; sponsors of bad deals may rightly fear they would be unable to pass SEC scrutiny.

Almost all real estate private offerings are specified, most often involving only one property. This makes it easier to conduct your due diligence on an offering, but it makes it incumbent on the investor to provide for diversification elsewhere in his or her portfolio. No one investment is so safe that nothing can go wrong.

In determining whether a real estate limited partnership makes sense for you, it is well to recall the disadvantages of the investment format: limited marketability and lack of management control.

This means that however much money you invest, you must be willing to part with it for a prolonged period of time, possibly five to ten years. If you have a balloon mortgage payment coming due or you are counting on the cash flow projected in the offering memorandum to cover your rent, you may be making a big mistake. Projects may not be sold when expected, or may not produce the hoped-for operating results. With your own real estate you can at least put it on the auction block well in advance of cash needs. Not so if you are a limited partner.

Another factor to be considered is whether you *need* the benefit projected for the investment you are considering. You may ask, who does *not* need tax-sheltered cash flow and capital appreciation? It is not so simple.

A retired couple in need of current income should consider a mortgage fund or unleveraged real estate, both of which are lower-risk investments with a high current yield. A younger couple with other sources of income can afford to sacrifice income today in favor of the potential for appreciation, investing in leveraged properties and possibly "value-added" or "vulture" programs willing to accept higher risk in the pursuit of higher returns. Not every partnership works equally well for each investor.

The Tax Reform Bill of 1986 created additional considerations. For example, is the partnership expected to throw off taxable losses or taxable income? Since you are considering a limited partnership, whatever benefit you receive will be considered "passive" in nature. Depending upon your overall financial planning picture, you may derive greater benefits from either passive losses or passive income, a topic explored in detail in chapter 13, "Planning and Profiting Post–Tax Reform."

For the most part, however, the type of real estate benefits you desire in a limited partnership will be the same as if you are investing directly. The advantage of limited partnership investment is that it gives you access to a variety of properties and a level of management expertise to which you are unlikely to have access in your personal investment forays.

Buying with the Best

Where does one go looking for limited partnership investments?

There are a number of places to find "prepackaged" real estate, and it is well to understand that the source of the product may have some impact on both the structure and quality of the investment.

Newspapers and the financial press. Only publicly registered offerings may be advertised in newspapers, financial magazines, and other periodicals. Advertisements fall into two categories—ads for products which are available through various selling agents (these offerings are discussed below) and direct solicitation from a sponsor.

The second category is our interest here. Like mutual funds, deals are often described as "no-load," suggesting that no fees are taken by the sponsor. This is not correct. There may be no front-end selling commission, but there is yet to be a publicly registered fund with no fees. The fees may be deferred, sharing arrangements for benefits may be tilted in favor of the sponsor, fees may appear elsewhere, or the total "load" may be lighter than for some other products, but there are always fees. If you get the prospectus, read it carefully and critically.

Another consideration in advertised offerings is whether the deal or the sponsor is really any good. Most of these products are unspecified, so you are relying on the ability of the general partner to buy the right real estate at the right price, and then to do something with it. The fact of the matter is that *anyone* can register a deal with the SEC and *anyone* can take out advertisements. Be sure you do not confuse good marketing with good real estate.

Stockbrokerage firms. Your friendly neighborhood stockbroker also carries limited partnerships. Generally, the firm will offer one or two private offerings at any one time, as well as a selection of public programs with varying leverage and investment programs. These private and public deals will generally have independent sponsors, with the stockbrokerage firm acting as *selling agent* in return for a selling commission and possibly a due diligence fee. The total of these fees is generally 5 to 10 percent of the capital being raised.

Some comfort can be taken from the knowledge that brokerage firms are obliged to investigate the sponsors and—where specified—the real estate being offered through their firms. It makes sense that they will seek the best offerings they can find. Your own broker may also have experience with the sponsor, having sold its products for a number of years and possibly having met the principals or seen a particular property. If you are going to invest a significant amount of money in an offering, you have no reason to be shy in posing questions to your broker. He or she will either know the answer or be able to get it for you.

Some of the largest stockbrokerage firms also put together and offer their own deals. This is both good and bad. The fees on these deals are rarely lower than the ones being charged by outside firms, so the offerings cannot be considered "wholesale." Also, while you may be comfortable with your brokerage firm and feel secure in the knowledge that they are intimately familiar with the real estate, be aware that their interests can conflict with your interests. Weakening market conditions have sometimes caught firms with substantial excess real estate inventory (e.g., deals acquired for syndication in the future). In these instances, commitments to independent sponsors are sometimes canceled. As a result, firms who create their own product may have difficulty maintaining relationships with top-flight independents, who require reliable outlets for their deals. Also, in these adverse markets, a firm with its own product has diminished objectivity about the quality or appropriateness of what it is offering. When tax reform was announced, it caught many firms with excess inventory—inventory which they later offered despite its reduced attractiveness under new tax laws.

Financial planners and insurance companies. Like stockbrokerage firms, financial planners and insurance companies are growing outlets for both public and private limited partnerships. Few of these firms are large enough or do enough business in these areas to undertake their own deals, so most of their offerings will come from independent sponsors. If you decide to work through a financial planner or insurance group, be sure that someone in the firm did sufficient due diligence on the sponsor and real estate, then do your *own* due diligence. The ultimate responsibility—and consequences—are yours alone.

The sponsors themselves. You may know someone in the real estate business. There are many fine real estate professionals who begin in syndication by offering their own deals directly to a local network of friends, acquaintances, and business-people. These are almost invariably private deals with a specified property acquisition. Some of these fledgling syndicators go on to form relationships with brokerage firms (who generally require that a new sponsor have some track record in syndication) in order to gain access to greater amounts of capital. Others never break out of the local syndication level because they are unable or unwilling to increase their organization to the necessary, stable size.

Investing with a sponsor directly often involves much lower fees than found in bigger, better-packaged offerings, but there is a wide range in the quality of the sponsor and real estate. One must be exceptionally careful when investing directly. Don't confuse sociability or friendship with integrity or real estate skill. The best and the worst syndications probably start near home.

Lawyers and accountants. Your lawyer and accountant, who should be advising you as you consider investments, do not sell limited partnerships themselves, but they are often in a position to see and review deals. Many brokers in my firm seek clients through professional referrals, so it should be obvious that good offerings can be found in the same manner. Even if only as a means to see more offerings for the sake of comparison, your own adviser is a good lead to what is available in the market.

Every single deal is different, so it would be impossible in the course of a short chapter to convey all the areas one should examine in an offering. Here is a checklist for some major items:

Real Estate
- Good location
- Competitive outlook sound
- Property profitable today
- Conservative projections (*Check those assumptions!*)
- Good real estate opportunity
- Reasonable acquisition price

Sponsor
- Track record in comparable properties
- Strong net worth (*Beware of hidden contingent liabilities!*)
- Solid organization
- Good references and reputation
- Guarantees for operating deficits and, if appropriate, completion of development
- Money invested alongside limited partners

Terms
- Sufficient capitalization
- Preferred return of capital and interest thereon to limited partners
- Fair sharing arrangements
- Fees reasonable for services provided
- Conservative tax positions

Need
- Suitability requirements met (*they may seem tiresome, but suitability was created to protect investors*)
- Investment affordable without strain or need for liquidity

- Yields superior to alternative opportunities
- Projected benefits consistent with tax and financial planning goals

This checklist is infinitely expandable and should be guided by the particular aspects of the deal being considered and by the final check of common sense.

The Future for Real Estate Syndication

Real estate syndication is and has long been, much, much more than tax shelters. In the first half of 1986, the year before tax reform was passed, 74 percent of sales in publicly registered real estate offerings were for so-called "income" programs with little or no tax benefits, a figure which had been increasing steadily for several years, and which continues to do so. In 1989, only a few percent of real estate partnership sales were in low income or historic rehabilitation tax credit programs, the only offerings with meaningful tax advantages. Still, changes in the Tax Code brought about changes in the way real estate is syndicated.

The most basic changes affect the way limited partnerships are structured and marketed. Some of the differences include:

Lower fees. Real estate syndication has a bad image, and real estate syndicators know it. With the tax incentive to raise fees and property prices gone, general-partner compensation levels have come down. The new marketing pitch is fairness. If it is backed by reality, so much the better.

Simpler deal structures. Again, the tax incentive to be complicated is gone. If you can't dazzle them with your footwork, win them over with an appeal to simplicity and logic.

Emphasis on real estate economics instead of tax losses. Obvious. If not because tax losses are harder to use, then because this is the *real* way to profit in real estate.

Less leverage. Leverage increases the potential for appreciation, but it also detracts from current income and generates tax losses. With less interest in losses and more in income, there is a decrease in the debt burden placed on properties.

New benefit emphasis. High write-off ratios and low net cash invested in programs are out. Deals are trying to provide early, meaningful cash flow to investors and an overall after-tax yield better than that available in other investments. Look for projected compounded after-tax yields of 12 to 16 percent in public offerings, a few points higher in private deals.

More offerings targeted to specific needs. Financial fine-tuning is the name of the game. Some products are designed to emphasize cash flow, others to focus on growth. A few programs provide passive losses to those who can use them, others throw off passive income (see chapter 13). More real estate is going into personal pension plans now that fewer tax losses are being given up, the main rationale being that real estate has less liquidity and pension assets are not drawn upon for many years. Mortgage funds—which happen to have some liquidity in many cases—are already a popular pension investment, and should remain so.

In addition to the changes in limited partnerships, some new investment vehicles have appeared on the syndication scene:

Zero-coupon bonds. "Zeros" are bonds where annual debt payments are added to the amount owed instead of being paid on a current basis. Zeros increase current property cash flow, a desirable goal for syndication of the equity ownership position in a property. It is likely that the debt position will often be syndicated too, meaning that zeros will be available with increasing frequency as a syndicated product. The risk is that too large a zero will grow faster than the pace of appreciation, so that the penultimate value of the property may be insufficient to pay off the debt. Like many things, zeros are good in moderation and are best when insured or guaranteed by a financial institution with a strong credit rating.

Subchapter S corporations. S corporations have been a traditional format for small business ownership, since they allow operating losses and income to be passed through to shareholders with no tax at the corporate level. Until 1982, no more than 20 percent of income could come from passive investment sources, such as rents. Also, losses were limited to one's investment in and loans to the corporation. With the 20-percent restriction gone and tax benefits modest after tax reform, the S corporation looks more attractive for real estate. Advantages over a limited partnership include ease of share transferability, ease of formation, and the possibility of more control over management for investors, all while retaining limited liability. Restrictions on the size and ownership of S corporations (particularly that there may be no more than thirty-five shareholders) make them unlikely to replace limited partnerships, but they can be an attractive vehicle for small syndications where a few investors wish to keep some measure of input to management.

Master limited partnerships. The MLP is really an old entity with a new following in the investment community. It is nothing more than a traditional limited partnership whose units are paired with "depository receipts" which can be freely traded on a securities exchange or in the over-the-counter market. MLPs are an attempt to securitize real estate ownership, a topic discussed in the next chapter. MLPs briefly proliferated post-tax reform as a means for major corporations to unlock and maximize the value of their underlying real estate assets, but quick action by Congress made it difficult to list MLPs on the major stock exchanges, tempering the activity in this vehicle.

Vulture funds. Less a new entity than a new strategy, vulture funds are limited partnerships that aspire to compensate for the declining tax benefits in real estate investment by creating spectacular returns. The strategy for this is to invest in distressed properties with the potential to be "turned around." If the sponsor is capable, this may be a good opportunity. Unfortunately, high fees in many of the vulture funds to date have had the effect of producing high-risk, so-so return investments. *Not* a good trade-off.

If there are conclusions to be drawn about the future of the real estate syndication industry, they would have to be that such an industry will continue to exist, characterized by a shifting emphasis toward simplicity and the quality of real estate assets. Good opportunities are there for those who would look for them and "buy with the best," but, as always, *buyer beware.*

CHAPTER 9

The Securitization
of Real Estate

For Widows and Orphans

Securitization is basically the transformation of real estate from a directly held asset to a freely transferable security. It is an attempt to correct real estate's greatest drawback, lack of liquidity. In the industry's century-long progression from a reliance on mortgage loans to the emergence of syndication markets, it was—in a crude way—approaching securitization. The emergence of real estate players with assets approaching or exceeding those of Fortune 500 corporations, the development of a professional management corps more palatable to Wall Street than the rough tycoons of yesteryear, and the continued flirtation of pension funds with real estate, a long-heralded affair which has never sparked the passion once predicted—all have drawn real estate and Wall Street closer together. Most recently, burgeoning capital markets hungry for new investment have combined with the growing cash needs of large developers to make the late eighties the age of property securitization.

At last, real estate would become as blue-chip as AT&T or IBM. Finally, real estate would be appropriate for the portfolios of widows and orphans.

This refrain has been heard before.

The stock market has had previous flings with real estate. The introduction of construction bonds preceded (but cannot be blamed for) the stock market crash of 1929. Many years later, in the 1970s, the market invested heavily in real estate investment trusts (REITs), only to see the REITs fail in a dramatic real estate recession. Even now, as Wall Street proclaims its commitment to securitization, we are witnessing the wreckage of savings and loan associations, which have overextended themselves with aggressive real estate lending.

Why are we doing this again?

Wall Street's current interest in real estate is far different from the earlier REIT debacle. The REIT was and is attractive to investors because income may be paid out as dividends without taxation at the REIT level itself (much like a limited partnership). To do this, the entity must satisfy a vast network of rules and regulations, most of which are intended to have the REIT function as a passive, long-term investor. As a result, most REITs in the 1970s were mortgage REITs, many of them created by major banks. The lending policies of many of these companies were overaggressive, often providing high loan-to-equity ratio debt on speculative development projects. It was the eventual, inevitable wave of property failures and foreclosures which brought the fragile house of cards down.

This experience left a bad feeling in the investment community. Even when real estate recovered and enjoyed a tremendous boom as an inflation hedge during the late seventies, many large financial institutions hung back.

Real estate did get some attention in the pension area, with large corporate and private pension funds investing billions of dollars in huge "comingled funds"—portfolios assembled and managed by major insurance companies and banks. These entities also alternated between catering to and competing with foreign investors, who perceived American real estate to be the most stable investment they could make. Real estate had clearly established itself in a narrow, rarefied band of high finance.

Some benefits were bound to trickle down to the public arena. Some of the same REITs which had failed in the early seventies were now prospering just a few years later, the value of their foreclosed portfolios rising as the boom in real estate increased the viability of even bad real estate. The publicity given to profits in some of these stocks began to again bring real estate to the attention of smaller investors. The climb of stocks for real estate developers and, later, of real estate syndicators, reinforced the message.

What is real estate securitization? It generally does *not* refer to so-called "mortgage-backed securities," which include familiar and long-established names such as Fannie Mae, Ginnie Mae, and Freddie Mac. While these financial instruments are ultimately "backed" by some form of real estate assets, such securities are either guaranteed or insured by a third party—such as the government, an insurance company, or a bank—and are therefore sold and priced based upon the financial strength of that entity. In contrast, real estate securitization generally suggests a direct reliance on the financial strength of the real estate asset itself. Hence, real estate becomes the basis for the creation of *securities*.

The pace of such real estate securitization has quickened, spurred in part by the recognition that real estate stocks dropped far less than the overall stock market during the 1987 crash. Standard & Poor's, the major credit rating agency, has begun to rate real estate debt. The implications of this move are tremendous, allowing real estate mortgages and portfolios of mortgages to be underwritten in the public markets. Public offerings have already been completed and many more are being planned. The prestigious investment bank, Salomon Brothers, expanded its real estate research area, indicating its intention to play a major role in this market. A slew of new products seems to appear almost weekly, as major developers and Wall Street move closer to one another.

Real estate is back.

Types of Real Estate Stocks

The real estate stock opportunities available to investors—either as new stock issues or as actively traded securities—are more than just "unleveraged real estate" or "mortgage funds." There are nuances to the way these funds are organized which are critical to their performance and what an investor can expect.

The most important of these parameters is the type of investment vehicle, whether the security is "open-end" or "closed-end," and what I term the *purity* of the investment.

Type of Investment Vehicle   Real estate stocks generally appear in one of three forms—real estate investment trust (REIT), master limited partnership (MLP), or corporation. As has been mentioned, both REITs and MLPs are particularly well suited to real estate because neither entity is taxed at the corporate/partnership level. In addition, both allow certain tax benefits to pass through to investors intact.

By definition, a REIT must invest in real estate. The laws governing REITs are lengthy and complex, but the principal features are as follows:

- Substantially all income must come from real estate–related investments.
- 90 percent of income must be distributed as dividends to shareholders.
- While investors have voting rights and control through their shares, a majority of REIT trustees (directors) who approve property transactions must be independent from day-to-day REIT management.
- With certain exceptions, the REIT is restricted to long-term, passive real estate investment. It may not directly engage in trading, development activities, or day-to-day property management (although "captive" management companies working only for the REIT allow considerable latitude).

By meeting these and other rules, REIT income escapes taxation until it is distributed to the shareholder (who receives dividends as *portfolio* income rather than as passive income, REIT restrictions notwithstanding). Because depreciation of real estate assets tends to result in *income* which is less than *cash flow*, the 90-percent income dividend distribution rule does not leave REITs cash-poor. Cash distributions above a REIT's income are treated as return of capital, and are therefore not taxable to the shareholder. Therefore, the REIT packs a double whammy—it escapes double taxation, and a portion of its dividend may not be taxable at all!

Master limited partnerships (MLPs) have also been discussed briefly. MLPs are limited partnerships (which have been discussed in detail in the previous chapter) which have sought liquidity through the listing of depository receipts (representing limited partnership units) on a stock market. MLPs have the same benefits and drawbacks as any limited partnership, notably flow-through of income without taxation on the plus side and lack of management control on the negative.

MLPs share certain benefits with REITs, but their differences are important:

- *The means by which each entity passes through income is different.* While the REIT must distribute most of its income and treats excess dividends as return of capital (thereby decreasing tax basis), the MLP must distribute nothing, *although the investor will realize taxable income or loss regardless of distributions*, and any cash distribution above the taxable portion has no effect on the shareholder's tax basis (any effect would be realized only when the partnership sold its assets). Also, related to the first point, *an MLP owner can realize a tax loss while holding his or her investment, whereas a REIT shareholder cannot.*
- If the necessary tests are satisfied, MLP dividends can qualify as passive income. REIT distributions cannot. As

will be explained in chapter 13, this can be a boon for certain taxpayers.

- *MLPs have virtually no restrictions on investment activities.*
- *MLP shareholders—who are really limited partners— have no voting rights or management control in most matters.*

These differences have combined to make the MLP very attractive to Wall Street. The individual receives more flexible tax benefits than a REIT can provide, while the issuing company or sponsor gets free investment rein and total management control. As mentioned, Congressional action has effectively divided the market between older MLPs with a grandfathered right to be publicly traded, and newer MLPs with limited liquidity.

The third form of real estate ownership, the corporation, is familiar to all as the standard means by which stock is issued and traded. Real estate companies organized as corporations are most often active operating companies emphasizing something more than merely holding a portfolio of properties. They are generally developers (creating or manufacturing product), brokerage firms (selling or servicing product), or syndicators (packaging product). All of these are investments more in the *business* side of real estate than in its assets, although these may be part of a corporation's value. With sensitivity to the underlying activities of the firm and its prospects in the current market, this is a perfectly legitimate means to invest in "real estate."

As far as the attributes of the corporation as a vehicle for holding real estate, it lacks the income passthrough capabilities of REITs and MLPs, though property depreciation may serve to reduce the corporate tax burden to modest levels. Investment flexibility is total and shareholders have whatever voting power their ownership entitles them to. If one accepts the premise that Wall Street does not fully understand real estate, some small value might be attributable to the familiarity of this most understandable of all securities.

Open-End Versus Closed-End   This is a distinction not found in most other securities. It arises from the portfolio orientation of most real estate investment. Very simply, an open-end investment is one which continues to make new investments over time. It buys and sells assets. It may seek new sources of capital through secondary stock offerings, issuing bonds, bank borrowing, or other means. It is an ongoing company, most often with its own management team. A closed-end investment is the opposite. Closed-end vehicles are formed to invest a specified amount of money in a specified portfolio of properties or in certain types of properties. The portfolio changes little over time. Most closed-end funds *can* sell properties and reinvest the proceeds, but few do. Any borrowing is generally for the management of the portfolio—perhaps to make a distribution to shareholders—not for new acquisitions. Most important, a closed-end fund is formed with a limited holding period in mind, generally seven to ten years, with liquidation of the holdings at the end of the investment term. The investment term has some leeway, so that investors do not suffer from poor property markets when it comes time to sell properties, but liquidation is always the ultimate goal of the closed-end fund. In most cases, management is provided on a part-time basis by a sponsoring company which probably has a series of closed-end funds and possibly other activities.

The differences between an open-end and a closed-end vehicle are important for the investor. First, it affords an opportunity to differentiate between good management and good properties. It is more important in an open-end portfolio to see good management, since the sales and acquisitions for a changing portfolio offer opportunities to maximize performance in a changing real estate environment. In a closed-end fund, competent management is important, but it is probably the quality of the fixed portfolio which ultimately guides value.

Second, the open/closed distinction is a means to invest in your expectations for real estate. If you believe the real estate market offers bargains to investors, your money should be in

open-end investments, which are continually in the marketplace, or in new closed-end funds which are now investing
their capital. If you anticipate that property markets will be
expensive, all real estate stocks will gain, but the closed-end
funds—particularly those nearing liquidation—will gain
most. The value of your investments will rise or fall on the
accuracy of your predictions.

The third consideration in choosing between open- and
closed-end funds is fees. Open-end funds with dedicated management tend to have much lower fees than closed-end funds
sponsored by another company. Closed-end fund fees are
comparable to those for real estate syndications. If a stock is
already trading, the cost of this "load" may already be incorporated into the price. If a security is in its initial offering,
the investor must decide whether these fees will hold returns
down below acceptable levels. If the investment opportunity
is unique—one reason why properties may be organized as a
separate security—the fees may be worth it. Hopefully, they
will be subordinated to some level of investor return.

A special case is the *self-dealing fund*, a closed-end fund
designed to provide money for other projects associated with
the sponsoring company. Self-dealing funds tend to have low
fees, but may be burdened by high conflicts of interest. These
funds are most often sources of mortgage money for other
funds or development projects, or they are net-lease portfolios
for operating companies, such as hotel or restaurant groups.
In the latter case, the net leases are in many respects another
form of mortgage debt, allowing the operating company to
do off–balance sheet financing and to concentrate on its core
business.

Investment Purity
What is investment purity?

An investment can be pure debt or pure equity, or something in between. The question of purity in real estate is in
no way limited to securities and stocks, but it is here that
the investor is most likely to miss it. And therefore, suffer
from it.

As a direct investor, you are very cognizant of whether you are purchasing a property outright, subject to a mortgage, or making a loan. Each has special implications for the nature of your return, and you are doubtless aware of what this investment is expected to yield.

The stock market is different. Pick up the *Wall Street Journal* or the business section of your local newspaper, and turn to the stock listing. You see column after column of little symbols and numbers. The true nature of the companies, their underlying activities, and their expected yields are rarely apparent. In addition, it is tremendously *easy* to buy and sell. If you are actively trading stocks, you may know very little about the companies in which you are investing. For most of us, it is impractical to do otherwise. One of the themes of this book is that real estate investment is a means of regaining a measure of that lost control that has occurred with the increasing volatility of the stock market. To the extent that one is going to invest in real estate *in the stock market*, I believe it is still possible to keep some level of control by *knowing what you are investing in*.

Investment purity is a basic aspect of that understanding.

A *pure debt investment* is the classic first mortgage. It has a fixed yield and term, no upside potential, and the first claim on the underlying property security in the event debt service payments cannot be made. A *pure equity investment* is unleveraged-fee simple ownership of a property (outright title to the land and improvements). Its yield is whatever you make after expenses, and you keep it until you sell it. Everything else is "impure."

Oddly enough, pure debt and equity are not opposite poles on a line from low to high risk. They are both "safe" investments, albeit with different yield characteristics. This does not mean that you cannot make risky debt or equity investments. Far from it. Loaning too much or overpaying are very good ways to lose money. *Investment purity is a means of characterizing anticipated yield and areas of risk, not risk itself.*

It has already been pointed out that real estate is an area notable for its creativity in developing forms of investment. Let us consider a few of these forms which, in addition to pure debt and equity, are most likely to appear as investments in real estate stocks:

Leveraged equity. This is equity, but riskier. It is the classic means of financing and owning real estate, with the surest portion of cash flow covering debt service and the upside going fully to the equity interest. With a steeper yield than unleveraged real estate and the risk of foreclosure in the event debt service cannot be covered, this may be more pure than unleveraged properties.

Junior mortgages. Technically debt, with a fixed yield and no upside; but second or third mortgages are "impure" and encroach on equity by exceeding conservative lending standards. With no senior lien on assets, one's capital is potentially at risk. The compensation for this risk is higher interest rates. You can call this a mortgage, but it funds the position ordinarily coming from equity. As such, it has aspects of leveraged equity risk, with a high-level yield replacing the gradual increase of cash flow over time.

Accruing mortgages. Like junior loans, accruing mortgages encroach on equity by providing more money than a property can initially pay debt service on, usually at a high interest rate. The difference "accrues" and is paid off when the cash flow is available. From a yield standpoint, this looks a lot like equity—income gradually increasing over time. Still, there is a limit on upside in the sense that when the accruals are paid off, whatever is left goes to the equity holder. It is unlikely that the property will be unable to meet debt service from one year to the next since interest is deferred, but it is possible that the eventual sale of a property will produce insufficient proceeds to pay off the accrued interest. The tendency of accruing debt to disguise potential trouble makes it a particularly risky form of investment.

Zero coupon debt. A "zero" is really just a 100-percent accruing mortgage. Risky business if one is not very conservative.

Participating mortgages. These are a true hybrid of debt and equity. Participating mortgages have a fixed interest rate—generally below the prevailing level on pure debt—combined with a share of cash flow and possibly of appreciation. In theory, these loans provide a minimum yield with upside potential, though not as high a minimum as pure debt or as great an upside as pure equity.

Net leases. We have talked a lot about debt with equity aspects. Net leases are equity with debt written all over them. Used in conjunction with corporate guarantees from the lessor, net leases are really corporate debts with real estate assets as the first line of security and corporate credit as the second. With percentage rents thrown in, the net lease is not unlike a participating mortgage. Investing in a stock comprised of such net leases, one should therefore look to the credit and operating prospects of the underlying tenants. If not for the tax benefits and the fact that the property value at the end of the lease must hold its worth (and hopefully appreciate in value), this might not be considered real estate at all.

Choice of investment vehicle, open- or closed-end nature of the entity, and purity are but a few of the ways in which real estate stocks can be categorized. Each stock will have its own blend of salient features. Most of the time, the important information can be gleaned from prospectuses and annual reports. Common sense use of this information is a good guide to finding securities which fit your investment needs. By the same token, common sense suggests that regardless of structure, stocks, management, and assets are of varying quality.

What is most important is to remember that all of those symbols and numbers on the financial page—real estate or otherwise—are not the same.

The Paradox of Liquid Real Estate

Real estate securitization seems inevitable, but it would be wrong to conclude that love is blind for Wall Street.

From late 1985 through early 1986, a new crop of REIT stock issues were introduced. Existing REITs were performing very well, and many of these companies sold stock to finance new acquisitions. At the same time, a fresh breed of professional-looking real estate companies saw the REIT— refined over the years to where sponsors could effectively work around restrictions on active management—as an attractive source of new capital. While the stock market wanted real estate product, its prices were often driven by investment yield. The problem faced by the real estate companies and their Wall Street patrons was that new real estate equity investments tend to start off with a low yield which builds gradually over time.

In other words, *real estate is a long-term investment*. It does not readily lend itself to situations calling for liquidity if that liquidity is based on income; current cash flow may not be a good measure of the value of real estate in the early years of a property.

By contrast, pure debt provides a high yield but no potential for appreciation. The solution hit upon by several investment banks and real estate sponsors was to offer REITs which would invest in participating mortgages. These loans had a lower current interest rate than "pure" debt, but shared in property cash flow and appreciation. A blend of debt and equity benefits.

This might have worked had interest rates not begun to fall. As rates dropped for conventional loans, rates for participating mortgages were driven down even lower. Few developers wanted to give up a large chunk of the upside in their properties unless they could either reduce their investment to zero or get a current interest rate far below that for a conventional mortgage. It became harder and harder to place participating mortgages at advantageous terms.

As a result, the participating mortgage REITs had trouble meeting promised initial yields of almost 10 percent. They began to trade at discounts to the offering price. Investors had lost money even though new entities were barely underway. Prices would eventually come back up as participation began to kick in, but why would anyone purchase a REIT in its initial offering if they knew it would soon be trading at a discount?

They were right, of course.

The same thing happened to new equity REITs, which attempted to substitute glamorous specified portfolios for current yield. Among the first of these mega-offerings were Rockefeller Center Properties and Equitable's EQK Realty Investors I. Both began to trade at a discount soon after being offered.

This came as no surprise to many real estate professionals, who had predicted that the stock market would evaluate real estate as stocks, on the basis of current earnings, instead of as properties, on the basis of a portfolio's potential for growth.

They were right, of course.

Real Estate Is Where You Find It
(and Money Is Where You Make It)

Where does this leave real estate securitization? Why, as an *opportunity*.

Real estate companies, like all companies, seek the cheapest money available in the capital markets to which they have access. If a sophisticated company offers a security in the public stock market, you can almost bet it is because they think the cost of that money is low. In other words, the public is overpaying. Not always, but often enough.

This is especially true of initial stock offerings in real estate. Be especially wary of companies created solely to acquire a specified (or unspecified) portfolio of properties, where lack of a track record and high fees may make it worthwhile to hang back. If the past is any indication, many if not all of these offerings trade at a discount in the after market (the "after market" refers to the interest in and price of a security in the period immediately following its initial public offering). The price at that time, since it may be based on an inappropriate emphasis on yield, may be a bargain. Prices are kept from getting too far out of line by the presence of large, sophisticated institutions in the market. Still, bargains do come up.

In the long run, the value of a real estate stock reflects the value of the underlying real estate assets.

This should guide your long-term real estate stock strategy. In the short term, any stock may move with the vagaries of the overall market, but ultimately, the value of the assets acts as a baseline for value. This is particularly true with closed-end REITs and MLPs approaching the end of their holding period. As the liquidation date approaches, these entities tend to trade closer and closer to their liquidation value.

For solid real estate investments, look for the companies that "stick to their knitting": established regional developers and REITs with a long record of performance. One tip is that the best real estate investments in the stock market will generally have their own management team. New entities under the direction of "advisers" are too often burdened by high costs and fees. If you are interested in such funds, consider investing in the adviser itself.

Before you go off to research what companies own what real estate, a word of caution: The share price of a few companies *already* reflects their real estate assets. In other cases, real estate may be an insignificant component of value.

Signs of hidden or undervalued real estate assets may include:

- Non–real estate companies with significant real estate assets, which are trading at earning multiples comparable to competitors without significant real estate assets.

- Old companies with manufacturing facilities—operating or closed—whose value may exceed that of the core business.
- Real estate companies—particularly long-established entities—with stock prices near book value, a poor indication of property values.
- Closed-end REITs approaching liquidation where stock prices have remained level.
- Small or closely held companies—real estate or otherwise—whose shares may not have been closely scrutinized by the market.
- Companies trading at a discount to their original offering price.
- Stocks with real estate holdings in areas which you think will enjoy strong growth, particularly where that perception is contrary to popular belief.

None of these signs are conclusive, but they suggest places to begin to look.

The opportunity for common sense investing in the stock market is finding the *hidden* value. Despite its overall efficiency, the experience of the stock market with real estate securities suggests that its pricing mechanism in this area is not as well refined as it is in others. If you can find a stock with undervalued property assets—*and the market eventually recognizes that value* (this is essential if you are to realize a profit)—then you will benefit from the securitization of real estate.

Part IV

The Investment You Live In

CHAPTER 10

No Place Like Home

The Biggest Investment

The desire to own one's own home is perhaps the single most pervasive financial planning goal—possibly even the most common *personal* goal—in America. There is less a question of whether a person will seek a home than of *when*. The considerations balanced in this decision include the size of one's family, the cost of a house, interest rates, and the level of other savings and purchases a person wishes to maintain.

Level of spending is crucial in the home-buying equation, since a house is the biggest investment most people will ever make. The national median price for a new single-family house was $92,000 in 1986, *up 385 percent from $23,400 in 1970.* In the resale market, the national median price was $80,300, *up 349 percent from $23,000 in 1970.*

These statistics suggest that single-family homes have historically been excellent investments. The compounded annual returns represented by these figures are only 8.9 percent for new homes and 8.1 percent for used homes, *but homeowners also have the use of their homes.*

This substantially changes the "yield." If one's annual rent savings (in this example, the rental cost of a comparable

157

home, without other expenses which would be incurred in any event) are just ten percent of home value, the return on a home purchased new in 1970 and sold in 1986 jumps from 8.0 percent for appreciation alone to *a compounded return of over 20 percent annually* once living-cost savings are included. This is a superb after-tax return by any standard, and could be enhanced even further by careful borrowing.

This does not mean that anyone who has ever purchased a home has earned a 21.4-percent annual yield on his or her investment, nor does it mean that the past performance of the housing market will be a harbinger of the future. It *does* mean that such yields are attainable and, since these statistics represented median prices, that even *greater* benefits are available to the shrewd home-buyer.

Certain markets will always be particularly robust at a given point in time. For example, prices in parts of the Boston and Westchester County, N.Y., markets advanced almost 20 percent in 1986, almost twice the national average and *doubling* the investment of a buyer putting down a 10-percent deposit in a single year. The challenge is clearly to find the market which will enjoy such growth.

There is a third component of return which must be considered alongside appreciation and living-expense savings. This is *use*.

As suggested in chapter 1, use is at the heart of the home investment. It is not enough to earn a fantastic return on our money if we have subjected ourselves and our families to inadequate living conditions in the process of doing so. The prevalent values in our society suggest that quality of life must have some value in the present, and few things impact our quality of life more than our homes.

Buying a house is therefore an attempt to straddle two possibly disparate sources of value—a good financial return and a good life.

Theoretically, there is no reason one cannot have both a good investment *and* a home that one is happy to live in. As a practical matter, this may be more difficult to achieve.

The process of finding and making investments is chronological. We look until we find the investment we wish to make. If we commit our money to a property, we may well miss a better opportunity which was around the corner; if we pass up an investment in search of a higher yield, we may never do as well. As a result, we find the ideal only if we are very lucky or very patient. Most of the time, we will settle on an attractive cost-benefit balance.

In house-hunting, this means we need to balance three factors—the cost of a home, its attractiveness as a place to live, and its prospects as an investment.

This is a dangerous mixture, as it may place emotions in direct conflict with finances. There is no way that the *love* one feels for a house can be eliminated from the buying process (nor should it be), *but it is imperative to recognize emotional influence and weigh it against financial considerations in a hard, steely-eyed manner.*

This may be the hardest part of buying a home—to understand the potential financial cost of personalizing value. If this can be done, it is possible to buy a house which is both a wonderful place to live *and* an excellent investment.

This is the ultimate goal of a successful home investment.

How to Find and Buy a Home

Entire books are written just on the subject of finding or buying a home. It is impossible to condense the technical information in these books to a mere chapter, so I will focus on the manner in which the particular themes of this book can be applied to the purchase of a house.

Key among these themes is taking advantage of market inefficiencies to realize superior value in your home purchase. This means paying less and getting more.

Here are some sources of inefficiency in the home market:

Divorces. When passions are high, prices get low. People anxious to get on with their lives or not looking out for the best interests of their spouses can result in below-market prices for the buyer capable of moving quickly.

Job transfers. Again, people pressured to move have more to

worry about than the last few dollars of value. In some cases,
their companies will be helping to absorb losses. Let their loss
be your gain.

People selling their own homes. This is a variation of the
unsophisticated-seller theme. Without the check of a professional, people selling their own homes are likely to aim way
high or way low. The houses priced way low do not last long
on the market. Obviously, the way to find a house "For Sale
by Owner" is to spot these words in an advertisement or on
a sign posted in the front yard. This means getting the weekend newspaper as soon as it hits the newsstand and constantly
driving through your target neighborhood.

Getting a house before it reaches the market. You may be
seeking a home in a particular neighborhood because you
know people there. Ask them whether they know if anyone is
getting ready to move. They may know of a couple near retirement or someone building a new home who has yet to sell
their home. Keeping a house from ever "going into play" is a
good way to keep prices down.

Buying off-season or where a seller is worn down. A relative
of mine had to move before his house was sold. Winter arrived
and the pipes burst, creating a flood which greeted him when
he visited the house. He was ready to sell.

Fix-ups. Many people lack the stomach or vision to buy a
house in need of substantial repair and work. If you can find
a house where the required work is only cosmetic, or where
the end result will be worth it, you may benefit from the
reduced competition. One strategy is to require the completion of certain items—such as a new boiler or a resurfaced
driveway—to be completed by the seller or as closing adjustments to the purchase price. You may get some of your fix-
up completed at an *un*fixed-up price. *Beware the fix-up which
is more than you can handle.*

Building. Constructing your own house has its own very special set of risks and joys, but it may be a means to get exactly what you want at a below-market cost. This may be particularly true in rapidly appreciating markets where a spread has developed between the cost of an existing home and the cost of land plus building, which tends to rise in a more predictable manner.

Cash. If you can manage it, there is nothing quite like the psychological impact of being able to offer a quick, all-cash sale to a seller. Removing the uncertainty of an offer subject to various contingencies can be worth a 10-to-15-percent reduction in the price of your future home.

Buying in bad markets. When prices have hit bottom, you may be able to find the house of your dreams for a fraction of what it would cost in a stronger market. Overbuilding, economic setbacks in your area, and high interest rates can be the cause of severe price declines. The typical pattern is that sellers initially pull out of a soft market, hoping to wait it out, then a few succumb to falling prices, then the market panics and falls apart. Not all markets go all the way to the last stage, so try to step back and do your own analysis.

These are by no means all the sources of market inefficiency which may allow you to buy a house more likely to hold and appreciate in value. Every market and situation is unique. Each will inevitably have pockets of opportunity. In bad times there will be many opportunities, in good times there will only be a few, but there will always be some edge available to the diligent, careful investor.

You will notice that many of the strategies suggested require certain common elements:

- *Strong familiarity with the market.* You can hardly buy below the going price if you don't know what the going price is.
- *A strong presence in the market.* You are not the only

bargain hunter. You have to see your opportunity and reach it before others if you are to succeed.

- *The ability to close quickly.* The probability of completing a transaction is in an inverse relationship with the time it takes to reach an agreement. This is proven over and over again at all levels of the real estate market.
- *Patience and flexibility.* A good investment cannot be rushed. The best opportunities are those which are seized when they appear. It is important not to delude oneself about the value of what happens to be available.
- *Real estate awareness.* The ability to recognize opportunities as they emerge, either in the overall market or specific houses, is an edge others will be hard-pressed to match.

These are the same principles necessary for success when seeking income-producing real estate investments. There is nothing about the desire to love a house which suggests that it cannot be a good investment too.

Applying the principles of common sense investing should yield a high return, both financially and in a house that well complements your life-style and personal needs.

The Last Shelter

Tax planning changed drastically with passage of the Tax Reform Act of 1986. Almost all deductions and so-called tax shelters were legislated out of existence. As a result, there is very little doubt that the home mortgage interest deduction is the most dynamic and important deduction available to the taxpayer in the post-reform environment.

TRA '86 also leaves intact: (1) the relief from taxation on home-appreciation profit when the proceeds are reinvested in a new home within two years of the sale of your old residence, and (2) a one-time exclusion of up to $125,000 in gain for home sellers over the age of fifty-five. These are two more incentives to own a home in a world with pitifully few other tax incentives. But nothing is nearly so important as the home mortgage interest deduction.

I call the home mortgage interest deduction a shelter because that is precisely what it is: the last tax shelter.

Most shelters generated paper losses for the individual without incurring a real cash expense, accomplished through the
means of depreciation. Home ownership does not do this, as a
person's residence cannot be depreciated. Home mortgage interest is a real cash expense, not an accounting convention which
distorts fiscal reality. However, the deductibility of home mortgage interest reduces the effective cost of debt to the taxpayer
and can serve to substantially reduce taxable income and, therefore, tax bracket. In this sense the home mortgage interest deduction is very much a shelter.

Trent, an investment banker with an annual income of
$120,000, and his wife, Caroline, have just purchased a
$260,000 condominium in Manhattan with $60,000 down and
a $200,000 mortgage for fifteen years at 12.5-percent annual
interest. Their annual debt service is $30,153, of which
$25,000 is interest in the current year. Consider the impact
with and without deductibility on their tax picture:

	Mortgage Interest Deductible	Mortgage Interest Not Deductible
Gross Income	$120,000	$120,000
Interest Deduction	(25,000)	0
Other Exemptions and Deductions	(11,250)	(11,250)
Taxable Income	$83,750	$108,750
Tax Liability	$20,175	$28,425
Gross Effective Rate	16.8%	23.7%

Congress continues to change (and refuses to clarify) the Tax Code virtually
every year, so tax rates, bracket ranges, and allowable deductions shown in this
and other examples in this chapter are subject to change. Individuals are advised
to consult their lawyers, accountants, or other financial professionals before undertaking investments affecting their tax planning.

Without the interest deduction, Trent and Caroline are
squarely in the middle of the 33-percent marginal bracket,

with $36,850 taxed at that rate. The effective tax rate on their gross income is 23.7 percent. With the interest deduction, their taxable income is sliced $25,000 to $83,750, where only $11,850 is being taxed at 33 percent and their effective tax rate is down to 16.8 percent. In both cases, they have incurred the full interest expense, but with interest deductibility there has been an $8,250 tax savings. In a very real sense, the after-tax cost of the mortgage is 8.4-percent interest ($25,000 interest, less $8,250 tax savings, divided by the loan principal). So long as the couple can earn at least this after-tax amount on their investments, it makes sense to borrow as much as the bank will allow.

The effectiveness of the home mortgage interest deduction in tax planning is even more powerful in the example of George and Sally, a two-income couple (he sells earmuffs and she is an earmuff buyer . . . a warm love story) about to purchase their first home, a Colonial in Webster Groves. Their combined income is $48,000 and the cost of their new home is $125,000, on which the bank has promised a $100,000 Fannie Mae mortgage for thirty years at 9.7-percent interest. Their annual debt service is $10,343, of which $9,700 will be interest in the first year of the loan. The ability to deduct mortgage interest is a substantial boon:

	Mortgage Interest Deductible	Mortgage Interest Not Deductible
Gross Income	$48,000	$48,000
Interest Deduction	(9,700)	0
Other Exemptions and Deductions	(11,000)	(11,000)
Taxable Income	$27,300	$37,000
Tax Liability	$4,095	$ 6,493
Gross Effective Rate	8.5%	13.5%

The interest deduction saves George and Sally $2,398, roughly equivalent to the commission on the sale of 12,000 pairs of earmuffs and 5 percent of their total income. Specifically, the deduction removes the entire $7,250 subject to the 28-percent marginal tax rate and slips them back into the 15-percent bracket. With mortgage interest deductibility, the effective after-tax cost of their mortgage is 7.3 percent. George and Sally's tax savings are $5,852 less than Trent and Caroline's in the previous example, and the reduction in their gross effective tax rate is less (4.0 percent versus 6.6 percent) because their tax bracket is lower (therefore, savings are worth less), but the percentage by which George and Sally's tax bill is reduced—38 versus 30 percent—is greater.

In any event, the joys of home ownership can only be enhanced by the knowledge that Uncle Sam is subsidizing you.

Borrowing Against Your Home

The home mortgage interest deduction opens another opportunity—and risk—associated with planning post–tax reform.

Under the old tax laws, consumer loan interest was freely deductible. *All* interest was deductible, regardless of its source. Car loans, financing for your children's college education, even credit card finance charges, were legitimate deductions.

No more.

Only two categories of interest deductions remain: investment interest to the extent it is covered by investment income, and home mortgage interest. By eliminating deductions for interest on other forms of borrowing, the effective cost of that borrowing is increased. This should be clear from reversing the loan example shown in the previous section.

The obvious solution is for the taxpayer to shift his or her borrowing for nondeductible consumer items over to increased borrowing in one of the surviving deductible categories. Since losses in excess of investment income are not deductible, there is no incentive to borrow against investments to the point where such losses are created. Also, bankers and other lenders are not easily persuaded to make loans secured by most non–real estate assets and will almost never make such loans beyond the capacity of the asset to service the interest. Therefore, the only remaining alternative is to increase one's home mortgage, where "income" and "excess losses" are irrelevant concepts. This is the basis for the so-called "home-equity" loan.

Congress, concerned that such loan shifting would result in waves of foreclosures against overextended homeowners, has attempted to limit the potential for abuse. Home mortgage interest deductibility is limited to the cost of your home plus any money spent on improvements over the years. This means that individuals who have owned their homes for many years are at a disadvantage relative to newer homeowners, for they are unable to tap the equity appreciation already built up in their home. The exception to this cost-plus-improvement ceiling is that homeowners can borrow to cover medical and education expenses up $100,000.

This is a loophole large enough to drive your car loan through. If you would borrow for your car but pay for college with cash, it is a simple matter to reverse your financing strategy. Monitoring the use of home-equity loans is a compliance nightmare for the IRS, although abusive practices and overly "coincidental" timing (i.e., home loan increased March 1, Volvo purchased March 2) are hard to defend.

What is the home-equity loan? Even before tax reform it was the fastest-growing segment of the residential mortgage market, growing 20 percent in 1985 to over $50 billion. Pretty good for a type of loan only seven years old. Plenty of room remains for further growth: The General Accounting Office estimated in 1984 that residential equity available as untapped home collateral exceeded $700 billion.

The advantages to home-equity loans are persuasive. Terms are five to fifteen years, compared with far shorter terms for traditional consumer lending. This results in lower loan payments, a benefit amplified by interest rates one to two percent lower than conventional consumer borrowing. Last but not least, once a credit line is established, money can be freely borrowed and used for anything (the fact that the use may or may not be deductible does not affect this), easily accessible by just writing a check or taking out a credit card.

The tax benefit of interest deductibility is reduced with the lowering of rates; but as it is one of the few deductions left, it is better to save a little than to save nothing. Shifting consumer debt to your home can make considerable sense.

It is still necessary to convince your lender that sufficient value exists in your home to justify additional borrowing, but how hard can it be to convince a bank holding the $8,000 loan remaining on the Jeep Wagoneer and the $3,500 debt incurred for Becky's braces that they should be willing to accept your *home* as additional security for your obligation? They would have to be foolish to say no.

Home-equity loans, which are really second mortgage credit lines, have typically allowed borrowing of up to 80 percent of your home's value. If this value is greater than the cost-plus-improvements deductibility ceiling, then you will be able to make maximum use of this deduction.

The increased importance of the home mortgage interest deduction invited the creation of a slew of financial products designed to facilitate such loan switching. For this not to have happened would have defied a tradition of opportunistic lending practices dating back to the introduction of loan-sharking. Such products—existing and likely to appear— include more complicated home-equity loans, high loan-to-value ratio loans, second mortgages with interest rate premiums, and even equity-appreciation mortgages, where increases in the value of your home—measured either through appraisal or national economic indices—automatically increase your home-equity credit line.

Such products will be tempting to many. Unfortunately, if the snake in the Garden of Eden were to be personified in the form of some modern-day occupation, he might well be a lender. With credit—and increased credit—comes responsibility. Responsibility for all that you owe. *Just because the banks allow you to borrow does not mean you can afford it.* There is definitely a perverse Peter Principle at work among lenders who continue to allow you to borrow up to the point of your insolvency. Someday I am sure a clever lawyer will successfully argue that the bad debts arising from inappropriate extension of credit to a client who borrows him- or herself into bankruptcy are the responsibility of the lender, not the borrower. The lawyer will not be entirely wrong.

The happy thought of a lawyer prevailing with such an argument is not sufficient rationale to indulge in the passion of *creditus non interruptus*. The stakes are too great: nothing less than the loss of your home, which is the security for all of your borrowing. It matters not at all that the bank's young MBA credit analyst concluded that you could afford an additional $15,000 of borrowing, or that you *believed* him. The result is still the same—foreclosure.

This brings us back to one of the primary tenets of common sense investing—*don't risk what you cannot afford to lose*. For most people, their home will fall squarely into this category.

Still, there are times when borrowing against one's home and loan shifting make considerable sense.

Suppose Dan and Phyllis purchased their home in the New York suburbs for $240,000 in 1984, taking out a $175,000 mortgage which has a balance of $161,000 today. With no improvements to the house, it has appreciated in value to $300,000 in the current market, giving them approximately $139,000 of untapped equity in their home, of which $79,000 falls within the cost-plus-improvements ceiling. Phyllis, a real estate agent, has found a one-bedroom cooperative in Manhattan for $100,000, which they intend to sublease to tenants and hold for its appreciation potential. Since a cooperative generally cannot be used as security for a loan, they put down $33,000 in cash and borrowed $77,000 on an unsecured basis from the bank where Dan works. Under the old tax laws, interest was freely deductible and they made a slight profit on the cooperative:

Rent at $1,200/month	$14,400
Less: Maintenance fees	(3,000)
Less: Debt service at 13%	(10,010)
Net Cash Flow	$1,390

In addition, they received a welcome tax benefit:

Net Cash Flow	$1,390
Less: Depreciation	(5,211)
Taxable Income (Loss)	$(3,821)

Following the Tax Reform Act of 1986, interest on the unsecured loan was no longer attributable directly to the cooperative. This results in the following scenario:

Rent	$14,400
Less: Maintenance fee	(3,000)
Net Cash Flow	$11,400
Less: Depreciation	(5,211)
Taxable Income (Loss)	$6,189

The cash flow appears to increase, but Dan and Phyllis still have to pay the interest on the unsecured loan, albeit on a *nondeductible* basis with *post-tax* dollars. In the 28-percent bracket, this adds $2,803 to their annual costs and wipes out their original $1,390 profit on the cooperative, which is now showing taxable income.

The solution is for Dan and Phyllis to increase their home loan by the $77,000 debt they had been holding on an unsecured basis, taking advantage of the $79,000 in deductible equity built up in their house. Borrowing this amount keeps them within the 80-percent loan-to-value ratio limit imposed by the bank's home-equity loan program. The interest on the cooperative is once again effectively deductible and, even though the loan cannot be shown to be directly attributable to the cooperative, their original income statement shows what they are really doing. For Dan and Phyllis, loan shifting to take advantage of the home mortgage interest deduction makes considerable economic and tax-planning sense.

There is no reason not to avail yourself of loan shifting for consumer purchases *if you have sufficient steady income to cover your additional mortgage debt service.* The family that derives its primary income from sales commissions or com-

modity trading should be more cautious about taking their
home loan to its maximum affordable level than a family
which looks to a salary and clips bond coupons. If you feel
you must borrow aggressively against the expectation of future income, it would be far better to drop a few dollars of
tax benefit and risk repossession of your car and furniture
than to flirt with the loss of your home. It is much easier to
take the bus to work than to sleep in the back of your car.

CHAPTER 11

No Place Like Second Home

An Asset in the Country

For some people, one home is not enough.

The second home may be a weekend retreat in the country, access to a warmer climate or a favorite sport, a way to visit one's roots and family, or a means to spend a surplus of money. Whatever its purpose, the second home is an asset, and few of us would gratuitously fritter away an asset or the investment it represents.

Consequently, the purchase of a second home deserves no less consideration than that given to your primary residence. There are, however, special questions which need to be answered:

- Does the second home satisfy a need which is durable, and can be expected to hold up over a prolonged period?
- Will it be possible to satisfy the maintenance needs of your second residence (everything from grounds care to turning off the water for the winter, if appropriate) for acceptable time and financial costs?
- Is the area in which you are investing one which can be expected to hold or appreciate in value?
- Does the price at which you are buying represent the

"intrinsic" value of the property, or are you paying a premium for market conditions? In other words, are you overpaying? If so, is this acceptable in relation to your level of use?

- Can you afford for your second home to *not* appreciate or, worse, *decline* in value? After all, you are using financial resources which could be earning money elsewhere.
- Is the second home a place just for you and (possibly) your friends, or is it intended to earn money? Is this realistic?
- Have you become so enamored with the romance, prestige, and convenience of a second home that you have lost perspective? *Does the use justify the cost?*

Does the use justify the cost? That is really the heart of the issue.

Most people underestimate the time and money required to maintain even the simplest second home. The investment may be such that you feel obliged to use the second home, forgoing other vacation spots which you prefer, if only for variety. Many people who would happily buy a second home would never consider purchasing income-producing real estate an equal distance from their own hometown. Remote maintenance can compound the difficulty of identifying and handling any problems you may encounter.

A useful exercise is to calculate the earning power that is tied up in your prospective second-home purchase. This will generally be comprised of the following items:

- Debt service, less value of interest deduction
- Maintenance costs
- Lost after-tax earnings on invested equity capital

It is not necessary to consider food or transportation expenses, as these would be incurred any place you might go. Now, calculate how many nights you can expect to use your second home each year—and divide that number into your total annual "cost." If the resulting number is substantially higher than the nightly rate at the finest hotel in the area you are visiting—as it often is—you should consider rethinking your decision to purchase a second home.

Despite the problems, a second home can be a wonderful thing.

It is a way to be established in a second location, surrounded by your own possessions and free from the hassles of hotel availability. If you can afford to be flexible in where and when you purchase, your second home can be an excellent investment. Here are several suggestions for ferreting out good values:

- Real estate prices in vacation communities tend to be more volatile than in other markets. Look for overbuilt markets, where prices may be depressed.
- If you have found your "idyllic spot" and it is not overbuilt, buy there. It will either stay idyllic and empty, or others will share your vision later, allowing you to sell at a profit when things get crowded. (One clue to which way things will go is how accessible your second community is from major metropolitan areas.)
- Buy in the country, just outside acceptable commuting distances. Prices get lower far from the urban hub. As suburbia spreads, your second community may become someone else's first-home market, with a probable increase in value.
- Buy off-season. Fewer things will be available, but there will be fewer buyers too. When people have to sell, they do not always have the luxury of waiting for the best time to do it.

If you are going to buy a second home, it may as well be a good investment. Additional help toward this end has been provided by the government, which allows several tax incentives to the second-home buyer. These are discussed in the next section.

Uncle Sam and Your Second Home

Second-home owners have the option of treating their second-home investment in one of two ways.

Option 1: Second Home for Personal Use   If your second home exists solely for your personal use, it is eligible for the same tax treatment as your primary residence. Mortgage interest and property taxes are fully deductible. This reduces your after-tax cost of ownership and offers an additional opportunity for loan shifting. Unfortunately, this treatment is available on first and second homes only, and may not be applied to any additional residences. Debt service on these properties is considered personal interest, and is not deductible.

Option 2: Second Home as Rental Property   Under certain circumstances, it may be possible to treat your second home as a rental property, getting valuable tax benefits in the process. This can be the case even if you do not think of your second home as "income-producing."

At this writing, taking a loss on part of your second-home expenses is subject to the following rules:

- Your personal use is limited to the greater of fourteen days or 10 percent of the total number of days your home is rented at "fair"—which is to say, market—rent rates.
- Personal use is defined as time spent in the residence by you, your spouse, your blood relatives, any equity partner in the property, any person with whom you are "trading" second-home use, and anyone who is not paying a "fair" rent rate.
- Time spent in the property for the "principal purpose" of making repairs or doing maintenance does not count toward personal use.

If these conditions are satisfied, you may deduct the portion of annual taxes, interest, operating expenses (i.e., mainte-

nance, insurance, utilities—just like any income-producing
property), and depreciation, that the rental use of the property bears to its overall use:

$$\frac{\text{Days rented at fair rental}}{\substack{\text{Total days of use (not including}\\ \text{repairs and maintenance)}}} = \substack{\text{Deductible portion}\\ \text{of total expenses}}$$

Therefore, if you use your second home for fourteen days and
rent it out at a fair rate for thirty days, you may deduct
approximately 68 percent of your total expenses (30, divided
by 14 plus 30).

This deduction is designated *active* (deductible against salary, dividends, and interest income) or *passive* (deductible
only against so-called passive income or upon sale of the property). To take *active losses*, one must own at least 10 percent
of the property and be significantly, legitimately involved in
management decisions. Deductions for active rental losses are
limited to $25,000 for individuals with adjusted gross income
under $100,000. Allowable deductions decline by 50 percent
of the amount AGI exceeds $100,000, therefore phasing out
completely at $150,000. Losses above one's allowable active
loss deduction, or not qualifying as active losses at all, are
considered passive income. A more complete discussion of
passive and active losses, what they are and how they may be
used, is provided in chapter 13, "Planning and Profiting Post–
Tax Reform."

Whether it is better to treat your second-home investment
as being exclusively for your personal use or as a rental property will depend on your own use and tax-planning situation.
The tax treatment of second homes changes constantly as new
laws are passed and the Treasury Department reinterprets old
rules. A final decision should await consultation with your
lawyer, accountant, or other professional financial adviser.
In any event, it is clear that a careful log should be maintained of your second-home expenses and use. To not do so is
to forfeit any deduction which might be available.

CHAPTER 12

When Home Is Not a House

They Don't Mow Sidewalks

Most of us can recall the time in the not-too-distant past when a home had to be a house.

Apartments were little more than way stations in the course of growing up, closets for one's growing possessions in the period between college and getting married. Of course, few newlyweds moved instantly to a house, but the inevitable push to save and purchase a house did little to alter the true status of the apartment as a place to wait for something better.

This is no longer the case. Apartments—whether rented or owned—have gained acceptance as homes for many segments of the population.

This was always the case in a few highly urban markets where there was a long-standing tradition of city dwellers, such as in Manhattan or parts of Chicago. However, demographic trends and shifts have served to broaden the importance of apartments.

Key among demographic factors are the tendency of people to marry later and increased divorce rates, both of which result in a larger population of single people at any given time. With greater economic resources than the apartment dweller of yesteryear, these people can often afford to move into a house, but choose not to because an apartment may provide better security, greater social interaction, lower costs, and—perhaps most important—simply because they do not require the additional space generally available in a house. A sixth factor, truer of rental apartments than of condominiums or cooperatives, is that an apartment seems more *flexible* than a house. With a high degree of uncertainty about one's future life-style and space needs, the very stability that once attracted people to a house may now serve to scare many away from this living option. If growing up is the act of making commitments, then perhaps personal commitments must of necessity precede financial commitment.

Another demographic factor which has long figured in the apartment market are the "empty nesters." As children move away from home and couples grow older, it is not uncommon for these people to eventually move into an apartment. This relieves one of home maintenance chores and expenses, and allows withdrawal of equity capital which may be built up in a house. Indeed, the financial motivation for exiting the house market is reinforced by the one-time, over-sixty-five home-equity tax exemption already discussed. While some older people have always "downshifted" into the apartment market, the increasing size of the elderly population has magnified the impact of this activity on the apartment market.

These are not the only events contributing to the new popularity of apartments. Among these are a revitalization of cities, which has resulted in more people moving to urban apartments, and refinements in the technology of apartment development—the apartment is no longer the depressing row of rooms remembered by some, but a high-quality living space with many attractive amenities. Some of the design and concept refinements in apartments were inevitable, but most have evolved in response to the demographic trends described, which created a clear demand for improved apartment living for an affluent user base.

Real estate developers enthusiastically satisfied this demand, constructing an estimated six million apartments in the 1970s, double the activity of the prior decade. This was 24 percent of the estimated total apartment supply in 1980 of twenty-five million units.

You may well recognize yourself in one of the demographic segments discussed here. If you do not know how or where you wish to build your life, if you want to live in the heart of a downtown area near thriving culture and nightlife, if you have not yet saved the money for the more traditional—and expensive—home of your dreams, or if you have merely grown tired of mowing the lawn, then apartment living may be for you.

Condos and Co-ops

It is possible to be a *home*owner without being a *house*owner. Condominiums and cooperatives—condos and co-ops—are occupied by millions of Americans, with the number increasing each year.

These are not just glass-sheathed high-rise and garden low-rise apartments. Condominiums and cooperatives can be multi-unit developments of any age or type. Once they were predominantly vacation homes, but this use now accounts for less than a quarter of all condo and co-op units. In addition to conventional apartment buildings, these forms of ownership are applied to town houses, row houses, attached homes, and even detached homes which are a part of planned communities.

This is because condos and co-ops are not specific types of real estate, but *specialized ownership systems*.

The condominium is by far the more common of the two forms. In a condominium one buys his or her own living unit, plus a share of the development's "common areas." This sharing concept is at the heart of the condominium. One's share is typically a predetermined allocation based on the size and amenities of one's unit in proportion to all other units in a project. The common areas are basically everything outside one's unit, from hallways to walkways, including a small share of the project's swimming pool, electrical wiring, roofs, and even dumpster. Any asset which is not part of someone's apartment is part of everyone's common area.

Naturally, one generally does not take turns with neighbors when the lawn needs to be mowed or snow shoveled from the sidewalk, though this method might be employed if the condominium was a two-family dwelling or some comparably simple building. Instead, there is an *owner's association*, where an elected board of trustees hires management and oversees the administration and management of the condominium project.

Obviously, it takes money to run an apartment complex. Routine maintenance must be paid for with distressing, perhaps maddening, frequency. As a consequence, homeowners must pay monthly *maintenance charges*. In addition, year-end shortfalls in the operating budget and unanticipated capital expenditures—such as roof repairs or resurfacing the parking lot—may result in additional *assessments*.

Paying maintenance charges and assessments is not an optional activity. Whatever amounts are set by the trustees or by a majority vote of shareholders must be paid. It does not matter that a person who does not play tennis does not wish to repair the tennis courts, or that you had a bad year when an assessment is made; the amount is an obligation, and failure to pay can result in the loss of your condo unit.

By the same token, you may be unable to convince neighbors that a new roof is required or that rosebushes should be replaced by tulips. Majority rules.

Similarly, condos inevitably have bylaws. You may not be able to own a dog, walk on the grass, or wash your clothes after midnight. It is even possible that having children will place you in violation of the rules and force you to move from what you thought was your home.

Being at the mercy of the majority is the major risk in condo ownership. It is not always recognized. In a well-constructed building or complex with an adequate operating budget, reserves for capital expenditures, and good bylaws, this may not be a problem. On the other hand . . .

Consequently, due diligence when buying a condo more

closely resembles that for an apartment complex than that for
a house. One must not only closely examine the unit he or she
is purchasing, but must also be sure to assess the physical and
financial condition of the entire condominium enterprise.

In buying a condominium, one is therefore confronted with
(1) the purchase price, (2) the maintenance costs, and (3)
ownership costs, such as utilities and property taxes, which
are paid directly since condos are owned directly. When you
are price shopping, comparables should be collected for all
three components. In high-quality developments, certain expense components may actually be lower than at lesser projects due to longer-lasting construction materials or thicker,
better-insulated walls. Generally, these disparities are more
likely to become apparent over time, and must therefore be
factored into consideration of newer developments.

A further cost is one's mortgage.

As condos have become more common, lenders have become more comfortable with mortgages on condominium
units. The rules for condo loans are much the same as for
conventional home loans, with a few notable exceptions:

- Interest rates may be slightly higher, to compensate the
  lender for the risks—to you and to them—that the condo
  association will botch up the project—their security—
  over time.
- Equity down payments may need to be greater than for
  conventional loans, for the same reason that rates may
  be higher.
- The number of available lenders will be smaller. Not *all*
  banks will make condo loans. Try your own bank or S&L,
  and be sure to ask the condo board whether one or two
  lenders hold an unusually large number of mortgages on
  the project.
- "Special" loan terms may be available. Many developers
  line up one or two "exclusive" lenders for the initial sale
  of a project. Sometimes the loan will come "directly"
  from the developer, a form of seller financing. In direct

contradiction of what would otherwise be the case, these start-up exclusives may have lower interest rates and require lower deposits than otherwise available. This may mean that the developer is subsidizing the loans. Such loans can be good things for the first-time buyer with thin resources, but look to see whether the developer is making up the difference in higher prices or whether *you* will make up the difference in higher costs.

In the final analysis, the loan is but another financial item to be factored into your analysis.

Cooperatives have some subtle differences from condominiums. Common in only a few markets—notably New York City and environs—co-ops are *indirect* ownership, whereas condos are *direct* ownership. Instead of owning their units, co-op residents own only shares in the cooperative corporation. Together with these shares, one receives a *proprietary lease* for the specific unit he or she has "purchased."

In many respects, this has the same practical result as a condominium. The only thing that has changed is that the living unit itself has become a special category of "common area" for your exclusive use. One still pays a purchase price for the cooperative shares to the former owner and one still has monthly maintenance charges. Still, some significant differences exist.

Because cooperatives are owned in consolidated form, rather than by individuals, the overall project may be mortgaged. This is especially relevant in projects which have been converted from a rental format, where cooperative ownership has allowed existing mortgages to be allocated among the co-op shares instead of being paid off. A co-op mortgage should result in a lower purchase price (since debt is "assumed" by new owners), but higher maintenance costs (since debt service payments are now included in this amount).

In addition to debt service, maintenance expenses also include real estate taxes, which are assessed on the consolidated property and then allocated. As a result, the interest and real estate tax components of co-op maintenance charges are tax-deductible. This tax benefit should be factored into your purchase analysis.

One of the disadvantages of co-ops is that it may be hard to get a mortgage to help pay for the equity portion of one's purchase price. Since the property is owned by the co-op corporation, it is not the shareholder's to mortgage. Any loan must be recourse to the individual, based solely on his or her credit and assets. Again, developers wishing to sell out new projects may offer special financial terms, but this too will be recourse lending with all its attendant risks. Cooperative boards will occasionally allow co-op shares to be pledged—and some lenders will even accept this security—but it is an uncertain, unwieldy financing proposition at best.

A special risk of co-ops is that the transfer of co-op shares is subject to approval by the co-op board. This means that you cannot freely acquire or sell your interest in the project. Co-op boards have successfully defended their ability to screen—and turn away—applicants who do not meet a building's credit or even social standards. Even more than in a condominium, you are at the mercy of your neighbors.

Outside of the New York market, the cooperative is rarely seen. However, it is not unheard-of and you must be aware of the co-op's special considerations should you ever consider buying into one.

The same opportunities and pitfalls for profit and appreciation exist in the co-op and condo markets as in the far larger house market. Perhaps more so. This is because the condo and co-op markets have been particularly volatile since they began to emerge as a serious development form in the early 1970s. Prices have zoomed in popular areas, only to crash in periods of oversupply. Buying a condo or co-op in a market trough—if it can be recognized—is probably more profitable on a dollar-for-dollar basis than a comparable house purchase would be. On the other hand, in a bad market prices for that same condo or co-op will drop far more precipitously than those for a house.

The opportunities and risks are compounded by the fact

that buyers and sellers alike tend to be far less sophisticated than in the commercial or "traditional" residential segments of the real estate market. These factors have combined to periodically draw speculators to the condo and co-op markets, where their presence has skewed prices further, confused the market as to the "true" market demand, and resulted in some spectacular failures.

The net conclusion is that condo and co-op investing must—as in all home buying—be balanced with one's living needs, one's financial resources, and one's attraction to the particular unit. If this balance is maintained, it is hard for the investment to be a *total* failure. Beyond this, however, a cautious approach to and study of the condo and co-op markets offers first-time home-buyers, second-home purchasers, "empty nesters," and speculators an area of acute market inefficiency and, therefore, an area with special profit potential.

When Renting Makes Sense

It is easy to conclude that renting an apartment, with its monthly demand for funds and no buildup of equity in any asset, is a waste of money and that one should purchase a condominium or house as soon as economically feasible.

This may not be correct.

There is no doubt that owning one's home is psychically reassuring. Still, it may not be the best financial option. If one's living needs permit deferral of a home purchase (which they may not), there may be opportunities to earn more on your money elsewhere. This may be true for you if:

- House prices are high, and you believe they will come down.
- You have modest capital and want to wait for interest rates to come down.
- You have a great deal of capital and want to wait for interest rates to go up, driving people out of the market and giving you a comparative advantage.
- You are starting up a company, and want to conserve your capital.

- Your apartment will soon be converted to a condo or co-op, and current residents—"insiders"—will be given a price break to encourage sales.

In such instances—correctly assessed—it may be more advantageous to rent an apartment beyond the point at which you can afford to purchase a home, entering the fray only when the market takes a turn to your liking.

Another instance where it pays to rent is where a market has limitations on the amount by which rents can be raised—*rent control*—thereby creating a situation where the cost of renting is less than the cost of a comparable purchase, even after factoring prospects for appreciation into the picture.

Peggy Nesbit has occupied her two-bedroom, two-bath apartment for eleven years. The apartment has a market rent value of $800, but rent control keeps her rent down to $550. To purchase a comparable condominium apartment would cost $80,000 and require monthly maintenance charges of $130. What is Peggy's true choice?

True Monthly Cost of Condominium Ownership

A.	Monthly interest on $64,000 loan at 10.5% annual rate	$560
B.	Lost earnings on $16,000 equity at 9%	120
C.	Monthly maintenance charge	130
D.	Real estate tax expense	50
E.	Total Monthly Costs	860
F.	Less: Tax benefit at 28% on interest and taxes	(171)
G.	Net Monthly Costs	$689

Taking tax benefits into account, condominium ownership is clearly more advantageous for Peggy than renting at the full market price of $800. However, due to rent control Peggy pays $550 a month, $139 less than the comparable condominium cost.

It is possible to argue that the lost earnings on Peggy's $16,000 equity investment should not be considered, as these are analogous to the opportunity for appreciation available in the condominium. This would make the comparison a far more even $569 for buying versus $550 for renting. How does one reconcile this difference?

Peggy should balance the realistic prospects for appreciation with the possibility of assessments or increased maintenance charges in the condominium, factors which might significantly increase her expenses. If Peggy's rent is lower than $550, if she can earn more than 9 percent on her capital, or if she has invested heavily in decorating her current apartment, it becomes more clear-cut that she should rent rather than buy. By the same token, if the financial equation and appreciation prospects favor the condominium, or if Peggy needs more space than her current apartment provides, it may be time to buy.

Every rent-versus-buy analysis is different. One must work out the numbers carefully, completely, and realistically before making one's decision. If you find that you keep introducing a bias toward buying, you may simply need to admit that the psychic importance of home ownership outweighs the greater return on your money that you could secure elsewhere.

Fortunately or unfortunately, living options involve far more than hard-boiled financial decision making.

Part V

Building Wealth in Real Estate

CHAPTER 13

Planning and Profiting Post–Tax Reform

The New Rules of Financial Planning

The Tax Reform Act of 1986 changed real estate investment in America forever.

There had been "major" tax legislation in almost every single year of the preceding decade, but TRA '86 was different. It was a watershed, casting off principles developed in the years since the graduated income tax was instituted and replacing them with a new set of rules. There will be new tax acts—representing both fine-tuning of the 1986 act and fresh legislation—but the basic parameters governing real estate investment for the next few decades appear to have been set down in the 1986 law.

This was legislation which would profoundly change the manner in which capital was formed and invested in America. The prior Tax Code—in all its complicated, unwieldly, loophole-ridden glory—was the incremental, if tentative, result of eight decades of using tax allowances and levies to incentivize and channel investment patterns, all the while bringing in sufficient monies to run the government.

In the tax system which evolved, each clause of the code had the name of one or more groups who benefited from the provision written next to it in invisible ink. These interest groups, whether organized, such as the oil or timber industries, or simply broad demographic categories of important voter segments, such as homeowners or the elderly, developed their industries and lives, corporate financial structures and individual financial planning, dividend payouts and savings plans, to be consistent with the rules governing the tithes levied as annual dues for membership in a great democratic club.

One economist called the new bill a "riverboat gamble" with the economy at stake. An equilibrium had been achieved and it was being tampered with at a time when interest rates were low and the stock market strong. Like the magician who yanks out a tablecloth from a table set with china, Congress was preparing to pull the fabric of the tax system, and America was holding its breath to see whether its dishes would topple and crash to the floor.

No group has been affected more by tax reform than the real estate industry, as indeed no group had benefited more under the old system. Cloaked in the flag, real estate had been the favorite son of the tax system. Maintaining the incentive to develop America represented the epitome of what the traditional tax structure had sought to achieve. Time after time after time, the government held out tax incentives for further real estate development, candy for a hungry, unreluctant child. The goals—all accomplished—were no less noble than the urbanization and suburbanization of America, the development of low- and moderate-income housing, and the revitalization of the nation's great metropolitan centers.

But opening a floodgate is not a precise policy tool. Together with the spring water came flotsam. Properties were developed merely to create activity, for the sake of tax benefits or marketing organizations or even for the sake of ego. Real estate was and is an industry bigger than life, with heroes and villains more heroic and more villainous than anywhere else in the world of commerce. Developers have locked in a race to construct buildings bigger, shinier, and sexier than any other structure before. In a nation renowned for entrepreneurial activity, largeness, and excess, no industry could have been more entrepreneurial, larger, or more excessive.

Then came the syndication business, an industry which was oddly populist in its marketing appeal. The syndicators marketed shares in real estate, pieces of the real estate pie priced from tiny slivers at a thousand dollars a pop to huge chunks costing upward of a million dollars. Packaged as a sound investment opportunity, the real product was a piece of the excitement. "Invest like the millionaires do," they whispered. "If they don't pay taxes, why should you?" How could one do any less? This was heady, patriotic stuff. "Buy a piece of America."

Still, this was populism for the relatively few. The considerable—and real—benefits of real estate investment broadened beyond the very wealthy to the fairly wealthy and even to the merely affluent. Amidst the hoopla grew a spiral of excess. Buildings were developed solely because land was vacant on which to build them, owing much of their value to tax benefits, to losses real and phantom which reduced the tax liability of those who invested.

The inequity was finally too flagrant to ignore.

Not that much money was really involved in syndication, relative to the overall scale of real estate activity, but it is the display rather than the reality of a situation which causes it to be changed.

Tax reform was and is far more than the elimination of tax shelters, real estate or otherwise. It is meant to rectify a breakdown of the federal tax system that reached into every nook and cranny of the code. Indeed, if the Tax Code was likened to a vessel intended to collect money instead of water, it would have had to be described as a sieve. One of the key architects of the code, Senator Russell B. Long of Louisiana, was fond of saying, "Don't tax you, don't tax me—tax the fellow behind that tree!"

The tree has been cut down.

Real estate was hit in no less than *eight separate* ways by the Tax Reform Act of 1986. In boxing, the "eight count" usually signals the approach of the finish of the match. It may or may not precede a knockout blow, but the *end is near* and the fighter rarely stages a comeback. The fit of the analogy was perhaps uncomfortably snug for real estate.

The Eight Count for Real Estate is summarized in table 7. Together, these rules reshape the tenor and form of all real estate investment activity.

The problem is that the open or shut gate is not a precise means to achieve objectives. The shut gate in this case is the disallowance of effectively all losses in excess of investment income. In its broad swipe at the addicts of tax shelters, Congress unfairly damaged the entrepreneurial middle class, which has traditionally used real estate investment as a means to bring in extra income and sometimes soar to the heights of financial success. The tax benefits in real estate afforded these modern-day carriers of the American spirit a means to break away from the inertia built into the tax system, with its tendency to hold people in their current income-tax bracket.

Picture the American people lined up in order of descending income. Tax shelters and other mechanisms by which assets are accumulated are means by which the entrepreneurial and industrious move ahead in line. At the same time, these devices serve to increase the distance between the wealthy and the rest of the pack. Tax reform seeks to compress the line by eliminating a major source of inequity in the way wealth grows, but at the same time reduces the means to get ahead.

In this regard, tax reform is very democratic, but it is not very American. As repugnant to our sense of fair play as it may be to allow others to butt in line, it would be even worse if each person did not attempt to jostle his or her way to the front. If the effect of tax reform is to cut the opportunities for the determined and entrepreneurial to build their assets through side investment in real estate, it would be a great tragedy indeed.

Fortunately, real estate as a way to riches (or more riches) is wounded, but not dead. Investment in property continues to be a preferred path—if not *the* preferred path—to the front of the line.

This is the case because—as this book has tried to make clear—property values owe far more to real estate's tremendous capacity to make money and to appreciate in worth over time than to any tax advantages that might have once existed and are now destined to be lost.

Moreover, real estate is not even dead as a tool for tax planning. The difference between financial planning and tax planning is simple. Financial planning is directed at maximizing one's assets over time, whereas tax planning is a specific type of financial planning in which the goal is to minimize one's taxes. There is no question that tax reform has reduced the opportunities for tax planning. Still, it never hurts to try, and a few tools remain with which one can work.

Balancing the Baskets

Balancing the baskets is far and away the most productive place on which to focus in post–tax reform tax planning. This refers to the so-called passive income "basket" to which limited-partnership interests, rental real estate, and other passive investments are relegated by the Tax Code.

This portion of the Tax Code takes the position that any losses in excess of related or comparable income in a passive investment may not be used. It does not matter whether this loss is created by interest deductions, depreciation, or real negative cash flow—it cannot be deducted against income from other sources.

Think of your income as falling into one of two baskets. The first basket contains: salary; portfolio income, such as dividends, interest, or royalties; and active investment income, such as the income (or loss) on a property which you are actively managing on a day-to-day basis.

In the other basket is income from "passive" investments. By definition, this includes all limited-partnership interests, rental real estate, and any investment in which you do not have primary management and decision-making responsibil-

TABLE 7

The Eight Count for Real Estate

The Eight Provisions of the Tax Reform Bill of 1986
with the Greatest Impact on Real Estate Investment

The Count	The Punch	The Damage
One: The Cut in Tax Rates	Two tax brackets, at 15% and 28%, replace fourteen brackets, ranging from 11% to 50%.	Lower rates reduce the value of tax benefits . . . and the relative advantages of real estate.
Two: The 5% Surcharge	From $43,150 to $89,560 for single taxpayers, and from $71,900 to $149,250 for joint filers, the marginal rate is not 28%, but 33%. This 5% surcharge brings the total tax bill for these more affluent taxpayers to a full 28%.	The surcharge targets the affluent taxpayers once most likely to avail themselves of tax shelter. It increases the value of tax benefits and yet it is hard to perceive and combat.
Three: Reduction of Capital Gains Exclusion to Zero	With no capital gains exclusion, all capital events are taxed at the same rate as a taxpayer's ordinary income, as opposed to the old top rate of 20%.	The incentive for long-term, relatively illiquid investments such as real estate is reduced without a spread between capital and ordinary tax rates.
Four: Lengthened Depreciation Schedules	ACRS (accelerated cost recovery system) and 19-year write-offs are replaced by straight line depreciation over 31.5 years for commercial property and 27.5 years for residential property.	A direct blow to the tax benefits associated with real estate.

Five: Extension of At-Risk Rules to Real Estate

Real estate was once immune from at-risk rules, but now only qualified third-party nonrecourse debt is deductible in excess of one's at-risk capital.

Not as bad as it might have been, it still eliminates several important standard sources of real estate financing.

Six: Reduced Deductibility of Interest

Interest *was* fully deductible, to certain limits, but now it is deductible only to the extent of investment income.

Another blow to real estate's solar plexus—taxable loss in excess of cash flow is not allowed.

Seven: Passive Loss Limitations

A new concept in the Tax Code, placing severe limitations on the use of losses from so-called "passive" activities (including limited partnership interests and rental activities) to offset income in excess of that from comparable investments.

Authored by the Senate Finance Committee—their attempt at a knockout punch: after reducing the tax-benefit potential in real estate, to stop just short of disallowing it.

Eight: Expanded Minimum Tax

The minimum tax under the old Tax Code was 20%. It is now 21%, but the $20,000 (individual returns) to $40,000 (joint returns) exemption is phased out at upper income levels. A host of tough new preference items make it harder to avoid taxation. Also, no transition period whatsoever.

The change-up. If you don't get them with passive loss rules, reasoned Congress, nail them with a stiff minimum tax treating most sources of loss as preference items.

ities, even if you have general liability or an equal ownership share with other parties.

Once your income falls into one basket, it may not cross over to the other basket. Therefore, even if you have excess losses in the passive income basket (the more likely place for such losses to occur), it cannot be used to offset portfolio income or your salary.

If real estate investment is your primary occupation or you are the sole or majority owner of an investment property, your interests do not necessarily qualify as portfolio or active investments. While TRA '86 expressly recognized the possibility that a property can go from passive to active or active to passive, the test is whether the taxpayer "materially participates in the activity throughout such year." Since rental properties are expressly designated to be passive investments, one might easily be fully committed to real estate investment and generate only passive income.

In a year where a property is under development, undergoing substantial rehabilitation, or is in the process of leasing up, it seems likely that even rental properties may be deemed active investments, but this is by no means certain. Presumably, in the absence of an audit or overwhelming proof, the presumption by the Internal Revenue Service will be that a given real estate holding constitutes a passive activity.

This new system dramatically changes the nature of real estate returns. Without exquisite planning, a real estate investor is far more likely to have excess losses than excess income in his passive investment basket. This excess loss is carried forward to future years and may offset any income in those years. The accumulated losses will generally not be fully depleted until a property is sold.

The key to using the passive income basket is recognizing that *passive losses are not disallowed on a project-by-project basis; all passive investments are lumped together.*

This creates the potential to build up tax-sheltered income within the passive income basket by balancing passive losses with passive income. There is no limit to the cash flow that may be generated in this manner.

All financial planning begins with using the assets you have. Assuming you have anything at all which qualifies as a passive investment, you will be in one of two situations: Either you have passive losses which you are in danger of losing, or you have passive income which is probably at least partially unsheltered.

Individuals with excess passive losses will include most owners of leveraged real estate, particularly those who acquired properties directly or through investments in limited partnerships over the last five years. A certain portion of these losses may be usable through application of the passive-loss transition rules, but less than half of these tax benefits will be applicable as early as 1988.

In order to use these benefits, the investor requires a passive investment which generates taxable or partially taxable income. Since the interest expense produced by leverage is the source of most excess losses, it seems logical to look for an unleveraged investment.

Naturally, one could go out and purchase a property with no mortgage currently in place, but let us suppose for the sake of this discussion that the investor turns to a publicly registered fund available from a syndication sponsor. In this case, one would purchase an unleveraged real estate equity fund, preferably one where the investments were fully or partially specified. This is among the safest syndication products available and, because of the diversified portfolio in which one is investing and the nature of the preferred returns usually available to investors, returns are relatively predictable and reliable.

After studying the available unleveraged funds, the investor selects Glass America Investors IV, an unleveraged equity investment in a fully specified portfolio of major urban office buildings (and a fully fictional entity created for this example). Glass America has an 8-percent preferred cash return to investors which is expected initially to be one-quarter sheltered through depreciation and to increase one percent (all unsheltered) annually after the second year.

The average annual excess passive loss expected from an

investor's portfolio over four years is $15,850. A $300,000 in-vestment* in Glass America made at July 1, 1988, will pro-duce approximately this amount of unsheltered income. Benefits from such an investment in Glass America alone would be as follows:

Year	Cash Flow	Taxable Income	Tax Liability	Net Benefit	Annualized After-Tax Yield(%)
1988 (6 mo.)	$12,000	$8,000	$2,240	$9,760	6.5
1989	24,000	16,000	4,480	19,520	6.5
1990	27,000	19,000	5,320	21,680	7.2
1991	30,000	22,000	6,160	23,840	7.9

Being able to use portfolio excess losses, which would oth-erwise be lost for many years until assets are finally sold, in-creases the returns in the following manner:

Year	Glass America Taxable Income	Portfolio Excess Losses	Net Taxable Income (Loss)	Tax Liability
1988	$8,000	$12,000	$(4,000)	$0
1989	16,000	18,600	(2,600)	0
1990	19,000	18,400	600	0
1991	22,000	14,400	7,600	448

The four-year tax liability has been reduced from $18,200 to just $448, a $17,752 savings which adds an average of about 1.7 percent per year to the effective after-tax yield for Glass America. The investor, by pairing passive income with pas-sive losses, has succeeded in saving a tax benefit which would otherwise have been lost and has maximized the value of a second investment.

You will note on the above table that no tax liability is incurred in 1990 even though there appears to be $600 of net

*The size of the investments in these examples is of no consequence. All figures can be scaled up or down to meet your particular needs.

taxable income sitting in the basket. Similarly, the tax in 1991 reflects a 5.7-percent effective tax rate rather than the 28 percent suggested by law. The reason this happens is because the remaining excess losses of $6,600 in 1988 and 1989 are carried forward, fully offsetting 1990 income and reducing the taxable portion of income in 1991 to just $1,600, on which $448 is a 28-percent rate.

In theory, your financial planning can even more accurately balance the basket in each year, but one is limited by the available investment opportunities. It would never be desirable to buy anything less than the best quality investment simply because it appeared to improve the fine-tuning of one's tax planning. In general, the best one can hope for is to try to use losses within a relatively short time of when they are realized. Remember that while losses can be carried forward to offset future income, they may not go back to remove tax liabilities from past years. Therefore, losses should tend to precede income for the maximum benefit in your planning.

The $25,000 Exception

One very explicit real estate tax incentive was created by the Tax Reform Act of 1986, but alas, it is not for everyone. The rule in question is a $25,000 credit-and-loss allowance which may be used in certain circumstances to offset salary or portfolio income. There are detailed restrictions governing the use of this allowance:

1. The source of losses or credits to be applied against other income must be active investment in a rental (non–net lease) real estate activity (e.g., no investment as a limited partner can qualify, and the investor must own at least 10 percent of the property).
2. The taxpayer must be an individual.
3. To the extent a taxpayer's annual adjusted gross income exceeds $100,000, the allowance is reduced by 50 per-

cent of that amount, but not below zero (e.g., above
$150,000 no allowance is available at all).

The reason for creating the $25,000 allowance is to recog-
nize that there are occasions where people are not engaged in
real estate investment for the primary purpose of generating
tax losses. Examples of such investments include rental of a
part-time residence, or of a previous or a future home, where
non-tax purposes are served but the effect of depreciation and
maintenance costs may be to produce either a phantom or a
real cash loss. Qualifying taxpayers may apply such a loss—
to $25,000—to offset income from salary or portfolio invest-
ments.

In addition, the $25,000 rule is an opportunity for the in-
dividual to invest in real estate even where it is not his or her
primary occupation and to benefit from the full tax benefits
traditionally associated with real estate. It is surprising how
much property can be controlled while only throwing off
$25,000 of annual losses. Suppose a property covers its ex-
penses and, if appropriate, debt service exactly with no extra
cash flow. In that case, the taxable income from the property
will be roughly the annual loss available from depreciation.
The table below shows the investment outlay under no-lever-
age and leverage scenarios which will result in $25,000 of
losses, assuming land (not depreciable) constitutes a tenth of
investment value:

	New Depreciation Rules (Commercial; 31.5 years)
No leverage	$875,000
50% leverage	438,000
80% leverage	175,000

Three things become readily apparent.
First, $25,000 worth of losses represents a considerable real

estate investment. *At these investment levels, no tax benefits are lost to the excess restrictions.*

Second, the use of leverage reduces the cost of investment to levels which are significant, but still affordable for a great many people.

Third—a point not quite as obvious—to the extent that the above property throws off cash flow in excess of expenses and debt service, losses are put to work sheltering that income, and even greater investment is possible without crossing into the area where excess losses cannot be applied against salary.

All of this is fully available to people with taxable income up to $100,000, with the phaseout beginning at that point; that can represent a very high total income indeed where the individual has availed him- or herself of the major deductions still available under the new tax code, such as interest on home mortgages and pension deductions. Also, *to the extent passive income is balanced with passive losses, there is no increase in taxable income levels.* Very substantial "hidden" income can be built up in this manner.

In most cases, the most difficult part of qualifying for the $25,000 rule will be satisfaction of the "active participation" requirements. This is a less strict standard than the "material participation" standard cited elsewhere in the code, and Congress specifically states that this was their intent. In the report of the Senate Finance Committee, where the rule first appeared, they wrote:

> The difference between active participation and material participation is that the former can be satisfied without regular, continuous, and substantial involvement in operations, so long as the taxpayer participates, e.g., in the making of management decisions or arranging for others to provide services (such as repairs) in a significant and *bona fide* sense.

It should be noted that there is nothing here which precludes the hiring of a management agent to handle day-to-day matters, so long as the investor continues to review and make major decisions and does not merely delegate what the report calls "independent discretion and judgment."

On the downside, it does not pay to get overly caught up in the game of maximizing one's tax benefits. With the reduction in rates, a $25,000 deduction is worth $7,000, a significant sum worth saving, but not an amount which should distort the entire thrust of one's financial planning. If this book has any point at all, it is that the proper rationale for real estate investment is the pursuit of cash flow and appreciation, not marginal tax-dollar savings.

Low-Income Housing and Rehabilitation Credits

The use of tax credits arising from investment in low-income housing and the rehabilitation of older and historic structures is the most complicated area in real estate taxation post–tax reform (as they may well have been in the old code), as well as the most subtle in their impact on tax planning.

Tax credits continue to be amounts awarded through participation in one or more of the few remaining tax-incentivized investment sectors which the government is particularly interested in encouraging and which it believes might not attract sufficient investment dollars without such incentives.

A tax credit is not an adjustment to taxable income, but an amount which directly reduces one's tax liability by the specified amount. This is an important distinction. A tax *deduction* of $1,000 is worth $280 to the individual, for this is the amount by which his or her taxes are reduced. A tax *credit* of $1,000 is worth $1,000, for this figure is sliced directly from the taxes one owes. In effect, the $1,000 tax credit is equivalent to a $3,571 deduction to a person in the 28-percent bracket.

Under the old tax system, the relationship between a credit and its corresponding deduction value was far more important than it will be henceforth. With fourteen tax rates, the deductions required to equal the worth of a $1,000 tax credit ranged from $2,000 for a person in the 50-percent bracket to a staggering $7,143 for persons paying 14 percent to the government. Of course, this is not a fair comparison since taxpayers who would have been in the 14-percent bracket—or the new 15-percent bracket, for that matter—are less likely to have significant real estate investment activities. With its multiple tax rates, the old Tax Code made investments with tax credits especially beneficial to taxpayers not in the top bracket. Tax shelters were priced to reflect the value of tax incentive to the highest brackets. This was logical since the main source of benefits—tax losses—were most valuable to those paying the largest percentage of income in taxes. Because tax credits work off tax liability rather than tax losses, but were still priced off the higher brackets, they were more valuable on a relative basis to people not paying the top rate. With fewer tax brackets, this distinction is largely gone. Still, if you can keep your adjusted taxable income below the 33-percent marginal-rate level with the use of deductions, credits will help your tax planning more at that point than they would at the very top marginal tax level.

Before concluding that credits may be your tax salvation, take note that they generally arise from passive activities and can only be used to offset tax liabilities from such investments. The exception to this is when credits are earned as part of rental investments qualifying for the $25,000 allowance against other income. In this case, you may not use $25,000 worth of credits, but the equivalent level of deductions, which would permit up to $7,000 of credits for taxpayers paying 28 percent, or $8,250 of credits in the 33-percent bracket.

Whether or not you have current passive income available to make use of credits, they are carried forward in the same manner as excess losses and should eventually serve to reduce tax liabilities upon sale of a property. Never pass up a tax benefit just because it doesn't look usable at the moment.

Tax credits are available from investments in both low-income housing and rehabilitation.

Low-income housing credits did not exist before tax re-

form, and are subject to a complicated set of rules. The thrust
of these rules was to take a plethora of programs which
Congress did not consider to be truly effective in promoting
genuine low-income housing (often resulting instead in moderate-income or even luxury developments), and to replace
them with one low-income housing credit which it is hoped
will result in affordable housing targeted specifically to low-
income individuals. The new credit steps beyond old measures, which focused on income level, by limiting rent levels
and tying the amount of the credit to the number of rental
units occupied by low-income persons.

There are five basic aspects to the low-income housing
credit:

1. The credit is claimed annually for ten years, with the
amount to be set so the present value of the credits is 60 percent (for credits applying to tenants with income at 50 percent or less of area median income) or 30 percent (where
tenant income is between 50 and 70 percent of the area median) of the basis attributable to qualified low-income units.
For projects on which construction commences before 1988,
the annual credit is 8 percent annually for the below-50-
percent income components and 4 percent annually for the
50- to 70-percent income amounts.

2. Credits are available only where at least 20 percent of
the housing units continue to be occupied for people with
incomes below 50 percent for *fifteen years*.

3. Only buildings which are newly constructed (and placed
in service after December 31, 1986) or substantially rehabil-
itated (expenditures over a two-year period of at least 22.5
percent of the project acquisition cost, not including land) are
eligible for the credit.

4. The basic amount on which credits are based is the lesser
percentage of the proportional number of (a) units or (b) floor
area occupied by tenants in the two low-income ranges to the
overall (a) number of units or (b) floor area, times the total
depreciable basis of the building.

5. The gross rent paid by tenants in units qualifying for the credit must be 30 percent or less of the qualified income ceiling for that tenant, an amount determined by family size.

The above litany is a grossly simplified summary of the actual regulations, intended partially to prevent anyone from concluding that the new Tax Code is really simplification and to indicate that qualifying for the low-income housing credit is no easy matter.

If this is still something you want, perhaps because the credit may be carried back three preceding tax years and can be carried forward fifteen years, it may pay to acquire a project already qualifying for the credit, since the credit is transferable if the old owner is willing to suffer recapture of credits taken to date or you are willing to accept *full* recapture responsibility in the event the project ceases to qualify within the fifteen-year term.

My own view is that you had better be fairly certain of the impoverished status of a neighborhood to make a fifteen-year investment bet. I am sure this is not the first law to create a disincentive for neighborhood improvement, but it is certainly one of the few. In any event, be sure to carefully consult the full Tax Code before undertaking either direct or limited-partnership ownership in projects aspiring to the low-income housing credit, then think about it again before taking the final plunge.

The rehabilitation of older and historic structures is the second area where favored investment status has been preserved, in this case through modification of an existing tax-credit system. TRA '86 provides a 20-percent credit for qualified rehabilitation of certified historic structures and 10 percent for rehabilitation of nonhistoric residential buildings placed in service before 1936. The credit amount is calculated only on dollars going directly into rehabilitation, and does not include the costs of building acquisitions, land site work, and most start-up expenses.

In general, a rehabilitation is deemed to be "substantial" and therefore eligible for the credit where expenditures exceed the investment basis in the building (e.g., the cost of the building, less land costs and depreciation) and 75 percent of the existing external walls are retained in place. In addition, the new Tax Code specifies that structures seeking the 10-percent credit must retain at least 50 percent of the external walls *as* external walls (preventing wraparound buildings) and at least 75 percent of the building's internal structure (preventing, though I am not sure why, "gut" rehabilitation that gives a new interior to buildings with exteriors worth preserving). Historic structures must run a gauntlet of applications and rules, ending in certification by the secretary of the interior, before the tax credit is approved.

Rehabilitation credits may not be carried back to cover past income and, unlike low-income housing credits, require a dollar-for-dollar reduction in depreciable basis.

Rehabilitation is one of the most exciting and romantic areas in real estate investment, and it is easy to get swept up in its excitement. It is also an area fraught with risks.

These risks include bad structural beams, surprises behind walls and ceilings (such as asbestos), and sagging floors. Rehabilitation costs are difficult to project, and cost overruns are the rule rather than the exception. Other problems, particularly in historic rehabilitation, include the difference between renovation and restoration (the latter is a far more costly undertaking), and the difficulty of securing timely feedback or final approval of plans and work by the secretary of the interior and the state agencies involved in the historic rehabilitation process.

I have been personally involved in both historic and non-historic rehabilitation projects, some of which have ended more happily than others. There can be no illusion that this is an easy form of development, but it can be a glamorous and rewarding path, filled with community recognition and personal satisfaction for saving or restoring a thing of beauty that is a part of the historical heritage of your community.

Undertaking either low-income housing development or rehabilitation projects is not recommended for the neophyte real estate investor, but both of these areas retain tax incentives in an environment where few such incentives continue to exist. As a limited partnership opportunity, these areas may be very advantageous to your tax-planning picture. In the end, the underlying economic viability of the real estate should be your final standard, for no amount of tax credits will be sufficient to compensate for the loss of your investment principal.

Real Estate After Tax Reform

It is clear that considerable tax-planning latitude is available to individuals through shrewd use of real estate investing. This is in addition to the pure and explosive *earning* power of properties. As a result, real estate continues to be the largest and most vital equity investment market in the nation. It did not sink into the sea, à la Atlantis, as many predicted it would after the passage of the Tax Reform Act of 1986.

It simply makes no sense to conclude that *any* measure taken by Congress could be the end of prosperity in America. People will keep living their lives, going to the office and the corner strip center. Nothing will prevent people from continuing to use real estate. It is this ongoing *use* of real estate which determines its ultimate viability, and with it its ultimate value.

If anything, the effect of tax reform has to be to increase the long-term value of real estate. By focusing the investor squarely on the intrinsic economic value of a property, and moving away from the confusion of tax gimmicks and complicated investment structures, more people will come to see the benefits of real estate ownership and begin to dabble in its delights. Increasing the number of players in real estate will increase demands for real estate, and therefore increase its value. *Can it really hurt real estate—or any investment which seriously claims to be viable—to be more intelligible and approachable?*

The specific provisions of the Tax Code will change with each new tax bill, and investors must stay current with the law or consult their lawyer or accountant, but one thing will be constant—real estate will continue to be a powerful, reliable financial- and tax-planning tool in the post–tax reform era.

CHAPTER 14

Investing for Profit
in Any Real Estate Market

Beyond Tax Planning

The previous chapter differentiated between financial planning and tax planning: Financial planning is directed at maximizing one's assets over time, whereas tax planning is a specific kind of financial planning in which the goal is to minimize one's taxes.

It is clear that a considerable tax-planning arsenal remains in the likes of the home mortgage interest deduction, the $25,000 rule, and balancing the passive investment basket. Combining all the available deductions arising from real estate will not eliminate one's tax liability, but it can hold even an affluent family to a low taxable income and put money in your pocket that would otherwise not be there.

However, most of the weapons in this war on taxation involve the commitment (or deployment, if you wish to continue the analogy) of capital to *assets*—in particular, to real estate assets with a longevity and potential impact on your financial condition far beyond one tax year. As a result, tax planning blends rapidly into financial planning. There can be no attack on the former that does not involve the latter.

In the final analysis, the decision to invest is a choice between available opportunities. The purchase of a stock, in-

vestment in junk bonds, opening a commodity position, or
acquisition of a shopping center, are each investments with
varying investment characteristics, returns, and risks. All may
belong in some part of your investment portfolio for a long
or short duration, but not all are appropriate for the investment dollar at hand, that amount which must be committed
now.

The destination for that dollar is the investment which provides the highest yield with the least risk while satisfying your
broader financial-planning considerations. Even if investment A looks better than investment B, you may still go with
B if you own a substantial position in A and feel the need to
diversify.

If you are like me, you will most often place your investment dollar in real estate. Due to the inefficiency of the
market, you will see the chance to achieve an exceptional
return—far greater than the alternative opportunities—at a
controllable risk while getting a powerful tool for tax planning. The component of value in real estate attributable to
tax benefits may be smaller than it once was, but it is still
greater than that available in other investments, and we have
seen that that is sufficient to wreak considerable havoc on
your tax liability.

No one would suggest that *every* dollar in a portfolio should
go into real estate. By doing so you would sacrifice some flexibility, particularly in the form of liquidity, the need for
which will vary from person to person. But you need not have
a diversification problem. Diversification by property type
and geographical market is every bit as valid as splitting
money between various industries or between stocks and
bonds.

Clever real estate investment can go far beyond property
itself. An apartment complex in Seattle is going to reflect performance in timber and aerospace—the main industries of
that city—just as the triple-net lease of a distribution facility
to a Fortune 500 company is going to have yield and risk
qualities comparable to a bond issued by the same corpora-

tion. The reason to invest in the real estate instead of the analogous stock or bond strategy is because the properties offer tax benefits and—correctly chosen—the possibility for superior appreciation.

It also pays to remember real estate's potential as an inflation hedge. This is not something on which we readily focus in a low-to-moderate-inflation environment, but a hedge is just that—protection against the possibility that something will happen. Like other considerations, real estate as an inflation hedge should be paired with the selection of property which will appreciate in value due to its advantageous market position or its acquisition at an attractive price. The marketing materials of Equitec, a large syndication firm, contain the admonition: "Investing is hard work, not high inflation."

This suggests the standard to which one must return again and again: to find the investment opportunity with the highest yield and least risk accessible within the resources you can bring to bear.

Creating Your Own Real Estate Boom

Buy low, sell high. Follow that rule and you can't go wrong. *But how tough it is to follow that rule!*

The problem, of course, is recognizing the top and bottom of the market. Given a choice of the two, one probably would (and should) choose to recognize the bottom when it presents itself. After one acquires a real estate portfolio—and is therefore in a position to be a seller—there is time enough to worry about the top of a market.

Bottom can be defined as that point in time where the maximum number of buyers are out of the market and the maximum number of sellers are in. It is at this point that market psychology and supply-and-demand factors combine to drive prices to their lowest levels. A careful analysis of this situation suggests that it is usually possible for the individual investor to recognize a bottom market and take advantage of it before more substantial buyers return to the market and take it over.

The situation that developed at the end of 1986, in a market reeling from the combined effects of tax reform and over-building in many cities, is an excellent example.

First, let us consider the behavior of buyers in that real estate market:

Syndicators. Tax reform decapitated an entire segment of the syndication industry, that emphasizing tax shelters. Having spent years trumpeting the benefits of real estate, syndicators changed the focus of marketing to "economic" deals, only to discover a massive credibility gap. Uncertain over their ability to raise money for non-tax-oriented transactions, most sponsors had to be cautious in committing capital to new property investments.

Lenders. Those who had provided the funds for the over-building of America were largely at fault for their current problems. Ignoring signs of a softening market and expecting strong rental demand to continue indefinitely, lenders had overextended themselves and made inappropriate loans in their mad pursuit to place money at attractive interest rates. Bankers and officers at other financial institutions are often reminded that they don't make money unless they put it to work in loans, but getting assets back through foreclosure became a grim reminder that nonrecourse lending depends on the underlying viability of the asset which is security for the loan. It was not enough for properties to ultimately cover the value of their loans, they also had to pay for the continuing debt service or provide sufficient reserves to see that properties had a chance to lease up to where they could pay their way. Even more guilty were the savings and loan associations and other aggressive lenders who indulged in 100-percent financing (denying owners a reason to sacrifice when the going got tough), excessive interest accruals, and participating loans, all made in the name of high income when they should have had high security in mind. The ill effect of these aggressive lending policies at the end of 1986 left lenders coping with

problem properties and out of the market for new investments.

Institutional investors. The managers of pension funds—and
even of some of their advisers—usually have no more knowledge of real estate than their own homes and perhaps a few
tax shelters purchased from the syndicators condemned above.
They too were guilty of buying properties that looked nice
instead of performing well. With ERISA regulations forcing
pension funds to adhere to a "prudent man" test in their investments (e.g., whether a prudent man would make this investment), these institutions were loath to be the first players
back into a market being described as "weak" by the national
news media. The risk-averse institutions would rather take a
chance on buying at the top of a well-regarded market than
to risk criticism by testing the bottom of a market in decline.

Wall Street. Despite the publicity surrounding securitization
and the anticipated surge in master limited partnerships
(MLPs), Wall Street was focusing on the narrow band of
credit properties and credit sponsors, which were not really
driving the real estate market as a whole. Most of the deals
getting done were for properties already in existence and
owned by the sponsors, and those parties who were on the
sidelines were waiting for the real estate market to recover
before entering the fray. In this way they could maximize the
prices which could be achieved in a public offering of stocks
or bonds. (This dilemma suggests that Wall Street is therefore
structurally incapable of capitalizing on a low market, for it
is in such markets that the Street becomes incapable of raising
substantial money for noncredit real estate.)

Syndicators, lenders, institutional investors, Wall Street.
This constitutes almost all of the nonindividual sources of
capital for real estate acquisitions. At the end of 1986, *these
buyers were forced out of the real estate market by the very
fact that the market was down.* And the forces that drove

them out meant that they would have to *stay* out until the market was already into a recovery!

At the same time, there was considerably more activity on the product side. Driven by the desire to avail themselves of low capital gains rates before the new tax bill took effect, many property owners ignored the depressed market and sold their real estate prematurely. More significantly, overbuilding forced the sale of partially leased buildings (called "see-throughs" since no tenants obstruct the view from one side through to the other) at discounted prices. Savings and loan associations, credit companies, and sometimes banks, who got in trouble through the bad practices described above, or through mere accidents of bad location, contributed to the availability of properties as assets became available through workouts, the threat of foreclosure, or bankruptcy auctions.

The situation was therefore one where many key groups of buyers were out of the market—*predictably* out of the market—while a considerable number of sellers were in. This created an opportunity for the individual real estate buyer who had the foresight to renegotiate existing contracts to more favorable terms and to seek new acquisitions at attractive high yields. With the economy in generally good condition and economists predicting the return of moderate inflation (a traditional boon to real estate), how could real estate have *not* been approaching the very bottom of the market?

It is in times such as these when the greatest bargains surface. There are *always* segments of the market which continue to flourish through bad times. There are *always* good properties which can be bought.

Bad properties cannot bring about a market crash. This is one of the most interesting aspects of real estate, that a poorly conceived property may never succeed, but it is unlikely to bring its well-thought-out neighbor down with it. Such projects are expensive to operate and profitably maintain, or are never comfortable for their users. Bad real estate is the reverse of an oasis, a dry hole in the middle of bounty. There are not a great many properties which are inevitably destined to fail, but those that are make little sense at any price.

This contrasts with properties that are well conceived, but make little economic sense. The most common example of this is the expensive, state-of-the-art project located in a market where rent levels do not justify the high development costs. There are quite a few such properties, primarily large office buildings, spread around the major urban markets. One of two things will happen to these properties: Either the current owners will absorb the costs of extended lease-ups and lower rents (with a commensurate decline in their return), or these errors in judgment will be sold at losses to new owners who, with a lower cost basis, will find their new acquisitions very satisfactory.

Overbuilding in the apartment market represents the same problem. The properties may not be overly expensive from a construction standpoint for their intended markets, but the press of excessive competition may slow lease-up or force rent concessions that raise the effective cost of development just as surely as if the builder had installed gold-plated faucets. Again, the choice is to absorb the costs or take the loss and let the next guy make it work. It is often said that real estate only makes money for its second owner.

Overbuilt markets represent situations where developers have done nothing more or less than build today what should have been constructed over the next three to five years. This is good real estate in good markets.

It is important to realize that it is not just the new and large properties that suffer in overbuilt or weak markets. Softness in leasing by the big boys is experienced as a downward pressure on rents and perhaps increased vacancies by smaller properties. For this reason, trouble in an area does ripple throughout *all* segments of a market, creating both woe and opportunity.

Eventually, virtually all markets will rebound from their problems. Sooner or later, supply-and-demand economics always exerts its authority. Market troughs and peaks are little more than deviations from the equilibrium established over time by supply and demand.

What is most important for the individual investor is that

he or she ignore the general consensus over whether a market is "up" or "down," "rising" or "falling." An investment is judged on its performance relative to the price at which it was purchased, not the market conditions at the time. *Nothing else matters.*

Investors must create their *own* real estate booms. The fact that this is possible is the great opportunity in real estate.

CHAPTER 15

Super Real Estate

Be Professional

The resources available to the prospective real estate investor involve far more than the time and money one is prepared to invest. The results one obtains will either benefit or suffer considerably depending on the *approach* one employs.

The question of approach is not the same as acquisition or investment strategy (although these too must be present), but rather it is the style and attitude with which investment opportunities are sought. This is not psychological mumbo jumbo. This is the essence of *professionalism,* and it is a crucial element in any success you may or may not have.

Professionalism is the façade presented to those with whom you are doing business. It is the way you dress, the way you talk, how good your manners are. This does not mean that everybody's façade needs to be the same in order to succeed. Just the opposite is the case, as true professionalism involves the ability to adapt to different situations—but it is important to recognize how the way you are will affect the people with whom you are trying to do business.

How you should behave depends largely on whom you are dealing with. You must judge the mood and needs of the situation.

Suppose you are trying to buy a tract of land from a farmer, which you hope to subdivide for single-family home development. If this farmer fits the classic profile of a farmer—down to earth, crusty, set in his ways—the last image you wish to present is that of the smooth MBA city slicker in a business suit, just arrived to do business with the country rubes. Down to earth does not mean stupid. *No* man or woman likes to be talked down to. Furthermore, the more you present the image of aloof wealth, the more you may inadvertently up the ante. By the same token, don't try to act like you were raised on a farm (unless you were). Such a negotiation calls for polite, straightforward talk. You don't have to present the numbers of how much money you expect to make from his land, but be sure you address his needs. I recently heard of one substantial and choice piece of land acquired for town house development at a bargain-basement price. As I drove through the countryside to look at the site, I saw a brand-new house in the middle of the fields, with an old woman knitting on the front porch and a shiny white Rolls-Royce in the driveway. Sure enough, the canny developer had recognized that the old woman who owned the land would respond to an offer of the house and Rolls as readily as she would have accepted another half million dollars. *Recognize whom you are dealing with, and adjust your approach accordingly.*

The approach suitable for working with an insurance company or a bank—whether buying or borrowing—is not much different. The plaid jacket that the farmer or even your spouse finds snappy will put you at a disadvantage with financial institutions. They are expecting a tailored business suit and crisp, businesslike manners. Without these, you are unlikely to get their money or cooperation no matter how good your concept or offer may be.

The exception to this rule is the successful eccentric. Real estate is full of them. The brash, unconventional developer/entrepreneur with his open shirt collar, rumpled appearance, and outspoken opinions is something all bankers have seen or heard of at some point in their careers, but it will not work unless it is backed up by a solid and checkable track record of success. If this does not describe you, it is best you not attempt the eccentric approach to professionalism.

Acceptable styles vary depending on where you live and where you are going. The blazer with no tie that works in Los Angeles or Tulsa is probably underdressed in New York. The cowboy boots that are de rigueur in Houston are maverick in Chicago. Some leeway will be given if you are from these places, but let common sense and observation be your guide. Conservatively styled suits are the uniform of the day in banks everywhere.

In general there are certain things which are considered professional *everywhere* and will only help your cause. These are:

Cleanliness. No one ever lost a deal because they had clean fingernails or good breath. I know of cases where these basics were absent and cost the buyers their credibility.

Neatness. Clean is not the same as neat. Many people in business feel that someone who cannot keep a crease in his suit would be incapable of organizing a multimillion-dollar development.

Good manners. Not kowtowing or effusiveness. Just "Please," "Thank you," "Nice to meet you," and "I look forward to your response." Businesslike. Crisp.

Straightforwardness. Buzzwords and convoluted presentations are out. Time is money and everyone appreciates a meeting that quickly gets to the point. Remember: Novels should build to the point, business discussions should *start* with the point.

Confidence. Don't be cocky, but timidity never got anyone to take a person seriously. If you don't believe in yourself, how can you expect someone else to believe in you?

These things all help to establish your credibility. The more credibility you possess in your own right through experience, net worth, and track record, the less important these other factors are, but they will never hurt.

There is a sixth area to professionalism which is of critical importance: *reputation.* Reputation encompasses several distinct areas, the most notable of which are credit, relationships, and what I shall for the moment call morality.

The need for good credit is obvious. In a business where money talks, your good credit standing is an objective voice on your side. Lenders, sellers (who must believe you will carry through on your financial promises), and tradespeople will all look to your past credit performance as an indication of your future behavior. The short-term benefit of delaying payment on a bill is a small gain compared to the setback if you forfeit your good credit standing.

Relationships define your ability to carry on in business. The first deal is always the hardest because you are likely to have no experience working with lawyers, accountants, engineers, and other professionals. In subsequent acquisitions these people and your experience with these people become anchors which give you stability. Like everything else, your ability to negotiate and close transactions will improve with experience. Working with the same people again and again, you develop relationships, learning where you need to be most attentive, correcting old weak spots, and gaining the ability to delegate more as the team you have assembled goes off to do its appointed duties with minimum need for supervision. It is hard to make progress if you are continually reinventing the wheel.

In the same manner, these relationships that you develop become your references for the future. Just as your credit can be a voice on your side, so can the recommendations of lawyers, bankers, and even sellers whom you have dealt with in the past. Your prospects are an expectation of your future performance, but your *credibility* is a measurement of your past, and those who have witnessed that past can help propel you forward, helping you to find new investment opportunities and to open new doors as you reach them.

The aspect of reputation which I have dubbed "morality" is very subjective. This is not whether you sleep with your neighbor's spouse, although this could certainly affect your reputation with some people, particularly your neighbor. Morality is the question of whether you are a *good* guy or a *bad* guy in business, whether you wear a white hat or a black hat.

I say this area is subjective not because different people will have varying opinions of what constitutes good or bad, but because both white hats and black hats, as well as all shades in between, can succeed in business.

Real estate is notorious for its wheeler-dealers, ruthless in their investment methodology and their treatment of people with whom they are doing business. I have been involved with many of these infamous moguls and can testify (sometimes unhappily) that their reputations are deserved, but perhaps misunderstood.

I know of few instances where the really top people in the real estate industry have actually *lied*. They are often vague and will invariably use their power (which derives from their control of money, the resource for which they are most often sought) ruthlessly to press a person to the smallest fee or share in a deal imaginable, but this reflects *their* sense of fairness. If you have the power, use it. They figure, with some justification, that if you could get the money or do the deal elsewhere, you would not be coming to them.

The lesson to be learned from such exchanges (as with sickness, one does not have to be cheated in order to take steps to avoid it) is to be specific and to pin things down in advance. If you have found an excellent bargain which you cannot afford and hope to find funding for it by securing a well-heeled partner, ask yourself whether that partner really needs you. If he does not, you may stand to lose the deal completely. This may not be fair, but it is the way things happen. Most of the people I know in the real estate industry have never subscribed to the "win, win" theory of preferred business behavior.

This does not mean that you too should don a dark gray hat, or that you should expect every person with whom you come in contact to try to cheat you. It does mean you should check things out for yourself, not put down money without protecting your position, and generally dot your *i*'s and cross your *t*'s—twice! Business is business and it takes all kinds to make the world go round. Forewarned is forearmed.

Pick your own moral approach to business according to your own conscience and personality, but do not be naive and do not renege on your word, as a reputation for this type of behavior always gets around and will eventually hurt you.

You Only Need One Seller

Developing your professionalism is really the last step in achieving *super real estate*, a state of grace in which common sense investing is raised to its highest level of execution. Super real estate means combining the best investment skills and practices together into a smooth, consistent pursuit of top-quality real estate investments.

Attention to detail, a thorough knowledge of the market, developing an investment strategy emphasizing your strengths, real estate awareness: There is nothing in these concepts which undercuts the plain, straightforward application of common sense. When you look at a shopping center or an office building, *see* a shopping center or an office building. Understand the activities which can take place there and consider all the financial realities behind those activities, but do not lose sight of what you are actually purchasing. The most important detail is grasp of the overall. This is the final and most vital investment check. The common sense check. It is at the heart of super real estate.

What makes a property good? The actual practice of super real estate and the purchase of real estate is the act of assembling, evaluating, and integrating thousands of tiny details. The particular factors you will need to consider will be different for every property—because every property is unique—but they do tend to fall into a relatively small number of recurring categories and situations which this book has attempted to highlight.

Here are a few homilies and acquisition pointers to take into battle with you. Most have been mentioned elsewhere in these pages, and none of them are very original—common sense rarely is—but they will serve you well under virtually any market conditions:

- Look for distressed sellers, not distressed property.
- Don't believe everything the seller tells you.
- Don't believe everything your own advisors tell you. Satisfy yourself.
- *Bad events.* Consider the improbable to be likely, and the impossible to be possible. Can you afford it?
- *Good events.* Consider the likely to be improbable, and the possible to be impossible. Can you afford it?
- Pay attention to details.
- "Location, location, location" is less important than asking *why* the location is any good.
- Are you buying below replacement cost (the cost of putting up the same building nearby) and comparable cost (the price at which similar properties have sold recently)? If so, is there a good (that means financial, not emotional) reason that this "bargain" is available?
- Financial figures—both past performance and future prospects—reflect real world events and circumstances. Understand them, and ask yourself whether your assumptions are realistic.
- Buy quality. Quality assets are the first to appreciate in value, and the last to decline.

- Be decision and action-oriented. It can be a tremendous competitive edge.
- Never feel guilty about buying below value.
- Ask yourself *why* something is available below value.
- Can you afford your prospective investment?
- Is the probable return superior to what you can get in alternative investments? At comparable (or acceptable) risks?

Work your way down this list as you consider the purchase of a property. Be sure you are satisfied with your answers. Pull it out again and go over the list just before you sign any checks. New information crops up during the acquisition process and deal terms change. It is easy to incrementally be drawn into buying a property when the deal no longer meets your needs. Don't let that happen.

There is one more very important item to always bear in mind—*You only need one seller.*

It doesn't matter if most properties fail to measure up to your (hopefully) high standards, or if the property you want can't be bought at a price you can afford. Most won't.

It doesn't matter.

With limited financial resources, it pays to be patient and wait for the properties that pass all of your tests with flying colors. It may be hard to wait, but in the long run it will be more profitable. More important, it will be safer.

Fewer surprises, less grief, more profit.

That is what super real estate is all about.

Get Rich Slow (but Do Get Rich)

Don't spend your money yet.

There is very little instant gratification in real estate. It takes time to find sound investment opportunities. Then it takes more time to develop and realize values.

The type of real estate investment strategy you choose to pursue—stock analysis and purchase, limited partnerships, acquisition for quick flips, acquisition for fix-up and facelift, land development, net leases, making wraparound mortgages to others, or an infinite number of other permutations on the real estate theme—will influence the speed with which your capital grows, but speed is not the reason to invest in property.

Invest in real estate because you believe that you can seek out and find those investment opportunities which will appreciate in value, giving you above-average yields with below-average risk. Any time you manage to break the relationship between risk and return, you are on the road to a winner. Ask any gambler. Tilt the odds in your favor and you may not win every time, but you will win more often than not and you will eventually break the bank. At Vegas or Atlantic City they would stop you before that happened. Not in real estate.

Applying the diligence and skills prescribed by super real estate, it becomes surprisingly easy to identify sources of market inefficiency.

It is unlikely this inefficiency can ever be completely eliminated. The sheer size and diversity of the real estate "market," jumble of locations and properties that it is, insures that it shall remain an inefficient marketplace, with careful research and due diligence creating the opportunity to achieve returns far superior to those available in other investments while reducing financial risks far below the levels one must ordinarily accept in the pursuit of high yields.

It is hard to succeed in the stock market, that most accessible and liquid of all equity markets, without being able to spend all of one's time following every pulse of the market. The money I have in stocks—other than a few real estate securities which I felt qualified to pass judgment on—is managed for me by expert money managers, professionals with access to the whispers that move the Dow Jones. Even that is not enough to prosper always in the stock market. I would rather leave the stock market to the few who are truly dedicated to managing money in that arena.

Real estate is and shall remain far more accessible and less capricious, a world open on an equal footing to anyone who would take the time to seriously research the merits of a given investment opportunity. The level playing field is what gives real estate its democratic character. The fact that so few ever take the time to seek out the properties with the most potential and the least risk creates the entrepreneurial opportunity in real estate.

Equality, but with the opportunity to get ahead through hard work and diligence. A return to the real American Dream. No stronger argument could be made that real estate remains the best and surest way to wealth in America.

While taking advantage of real estate's inefficiency, investors must at the same time be wary of the sometimes rapid changes which afflict real estate. This changing nature can never be ignored. Change is implicit in both the property life cycle and the cyclical nature of the industry itself. Just as real estate awareness is a habit by which new opportunities are recognized, so is it a means by which new traps and the disappearance of obsolete forms are spotted before they hurt you.

All of this has to be implicit in your approach to investment. A good investment strategy has five ingredients:

1. Consistency with financial resources.
2. Consistency with time and organizational resources.
3. Consistency with the market.
4. Direction—it must lead somewhere.
5. Periodic review for change—change with the times. If you are the last to abandon an old position and last to embrace a new investment mode, you are almost certainly too late on both counts.

This is super real estate. It facilitates buying low and selling high. *It takes advantage of change.*

This is not an easy thing to do, but it is not impossible either. The tendency toward change in real estate is best capitalized upon by never losing sight of how properties are *used*. That is the nice thing about real estate—its use is a reflection of the way people live, something everyone is capable of observing. After all, who is *not* an expert in the way people live?

If change is the first and main continuing theme in real estate, creativity is probably the second. Change opens the door for creativity.

The real estate market may be inefficient on a property-by-property basis, but it is sufficiently efficient overall to close off old ideas over time, necessitating new approaches. Never become too attached to one formula, because the formula changes. The more refined your strategy, the more it depends on a single niche, the more likely you will need to evolve and change. Everyone has had an itch which seems to move when you scratch it. *You* have to move too. The only constants in your real estate investment strategy should be common sense, the accumulation of profit, and a bias toward *action*.

You can make fortunes on paper or in your head, but if you don't put your money where your desires are, it will make no difference for you at the bank. To *act* upon your ambitions is the key. In 1859, George Eliot wrote, "It's them that take advantage that get advantage i' this world." It is not enough to *have* common sense if one does not *use* common sense.

Whether real estate is going to be 10 percent or 90 percent of your investment portfolio, it is a block of capital that, properly nurtured, will grow and bear fruit over time.

It is well established that real estate makes money and money makes fortunes, and that is a very sweet fruit indeed.

Index

Texas Instruments
  Business Analyst, 89
Timing, 61
Total return ratio, 92
Transferability, 138, 140
  co-op shares, 182
  tax credits, 205
Treasury bills, 6, 7 (table)
Turnover rates, 21–22, 62
$25,000 rule, 209

U.S. Bureau of Economics, 71
U.S. Congress, 3, 166, 190, 192
  Senate Finance Committee, 201
Unspecified offering, 128, 132, 152
Upside, 149, 151
Urban growth, 61, 65
Use, 16, 75, 226–27
  of home, 148
  of second home, 172, 174, 175
User perspective, 42–44

Vacancy(ies), 21–22, 28
Value, 47, 48, 207–8, 210
  creation of, 61, 62, 77
  effect of future events on current, 87
  land, 30–31, 43, 61

personalization of, 159
present, 88–91, 92
property, 193
real estate stocks, 153
VMS Realty, 65–66
Vulture funds, 139

Wage index, 6, 7 (table)
Wall Street, 213
  see also Stock market
Westchester County (N.Y.), 158
Worth (property), 84

Yield, 47, 49, 78, 92–93, 151, 152, 210
  above-market, 79
  after-tax, 34
  in home-buying, 157–58
  investment purity and, 148
  leverage and, 110–12
  limited partnerships, 136
  market strength and, 74, 75
  measurement of, 92
  minimum, 49
  overall, 86–91
  participating mortgages, 150

Zero-coupon bonds ("zeros"), 137–38
Zero coupon debt, 150